69

Obama Lies

Deceptions and Attacks on Our
Constitution and Way of Life

Grassfire Nation

Printed in the United States of America

First Printing, 2012

ISBN 0-9849860-1-9

Grassfire Nation
PO Box 277
Maxwell, IA 50161
www.Grassfire.com

About Grassfire Nation

Grassfire Nation, a division of Grassroots Action,
Inc., is a million-strong network of grassroots
conservatives dedicated to equipping you with the
tools that give you a real impact on the key issues of
our day. We also operate a social networking site
(PatriotActionNetwork.com) and a patriot-sourced
news website (LibertyNews.com).

Table Of Contents

There Are Lies, Damned Lies, And ObamaLies

"All men having power ought to be distrusted," said James Madison who, like all the founders, harbored healthy skepticism about the ability of mere mortals to rule well in the absence of a system to check and diffuse power. Well, we saw in 2009-2010 what happens when power is unchecked as President Obama, in league with a Democrat-controlled Congress, went on a historic spending binge and brought health care, one sixth of the U.S. economy, under government control.

The remarkable legislative record of Obama's first two years points to one of the campaign promises which he did keep — and then some: "We are five days away from fundamentally transforming the United States of America."

But that on-going transformation, detailed in our earlier handbook, *Obama Exposed: 21 Ways Barack Obama is Radically Re-Shaping America In His Own Image,* hasn't come easy for Obama (and certainly not for the nation). A gifted politician with an intriguing personal story, Obama has, more than most politicians, had to rely on a mix of distortions, deceptions, and downright lies to bend voters to his will.

It has worked all too well.

Obama won the White House and, later, his signature legislative achievement, ObamaCare, in large part on his capacity to tell stories and assert claims that shade or distort the truth or, sometimes, just make it up. And he's been able to do so in large part because of a friendly media which has failed to dig into his past or ask him hard questions about his days as a community organizer in Chicago or his many troubling associations of which the angry and venomous Rev. Jeremiah Wright was just one.

The media's pattern of protective responses to damaging information about Obama has persisted into his presidency. Their dismissive yawn when Breitbart.com surfaced suppressed video showing a young Obama praising Derrick Bell, an influential academic who regarded our nation as hopelessly riddled with racism, is one recent example.

From Obama's perspective, it makes perfect sense that he has kept much of his past career as a community organizer in the shadows and used charm and guile to airbrush a false image of himself and his aims in his books, speeches, and interviews. He has much to hide both as to history and agenda.

Just think about the rogue's gallery of friends and associates in his past:

- Rev. Wright, whose tirade against the alleged racist sins of America and call for God to "damn America" shocked the nation and almost derailed Obama's bid for the White House.

- Bill Ayers and Bernardine Dohrn, unrepentant domestic terrorists who spent years on the lam before reinventing themselves as academics and settling into Chicago's Hyde Park neighborhood.

2   *Grassfire Nation*

- Father Michael Pfleger, a far-left priest, admirer of Louis Farrakhan, and close friend to Obama.

- ACORN, the radical community organizing group with which Obama worked while in Chicago.

Until some "citizen journalists" began digging, not much was known about these connections. The opacity of Obama's past contrasts sharply with his promise to have the most transparent administration in history.

But it wasn't just his past that Obama had to hide from prying eyes (or not so prying, in the case of the media). It was also his policies. On spending, health care, lobbyists, transparency, Israel, Islam, immigration, energy, and more, Obama has found it necessary to cloak his aims, or the truth of their outcome, in lies.

One example. It seems incredible now, but Obama cast himself as a deficit hawk on his way to the White House. He promised to cut the deficit in half by the end of his four-year term and said he would go "line by line" through the budget to eliminate pork. Instead, Obama has added $5 trillion in debt in just over 3 years in office.

This is one of the first compendiums of the lies of Barack – and it's by no means complete. The lies just keep coming, and the tempo will likely quicken as we approach what is one of the most consequential elections in U.S. history. *69 Obama Lies* offers a disturbing cross-section of the fibs, falsehoods, and fabrications that our President has used to win votes and remain popular, even as his policies bring weakness abroad, high unemployment, sluggish economic growth, and more big government into American life.

69 Obama Lies highlights the wisdom of Madison's words: "All men having power ought to be distrusted." It also brings to mind the words of Mark Twain, a man who may have understood our nation's psyche as well as any American in our history. He saw in everyday life the power of the spoken word and the ability to deceive by use of facts, figures and language. "There are three kinds of lies: lies, damned lies, and statistics," he wrote in *Chapters from my Autobiography.* Twain may have understood the American mind, but he never met Barack Hussein Obama.

Let us introduce you to him anew.

In our therapeutic and PC world, it's not well thought of to accuse someone of dishonesty, as Rep. Joe Wilson discovered when he shouted to President Barack Obama, "You lie!" during Obama's 2010 State of the Union address. (Wilson was correct, as you'll discover.) Still, "Facts are stubborn things," as John Adams famously said, and that's why we've produced this powerful expose. It strips away the veneer of lies and gives you, in disturbing detail, the facts about this man and his mendacity.

Section One
ObamaLies

When chronicling the Obama Lies, the logical place to start is with the man himself. When a person lies about who he is, what he believes and whom he has associated with, at a fundamental level, he becomes a lie. Welcome to the world of Barack Obama and the series of ObamaLies which paved the way for this Marxist community organizer to get elected in the first place. Lest we forget, here's a quick review of the lies which reveal the true character and beliefs of the man who had to deny who he fundamentally is and his core relationships in order to win the presidency. The ObamaLies.

1

The "I'm Not a Socialist" LIE

"The answer would be no." —BHO
(in response to being asked if he is a socialist.)

President Obama called reporters in March 2009 to make sure they knew that, no, he is not a socialist.[1] Well, let's take a look at what he's said and done. He never tires of calling for more taxes on the "rich," and did tell Joe the Plumber, that "when you spread the wealth around, it's good for everybody." And his signature first-term legislative achievement,

ObamaCare, puts the health care industry, 18 percent of the American economy, under direct control of the federal government. The control is so complete that the law empowers Health and Human Services Secretary Kathleen Sebelius to force health insurance providers to offer free contraceptives, including abortion causing drugs, directly to the employees of firms for which they provide insurance — even if such a mandate violates the moral consciences of employers and workers forced to pay for the health plans.

We are in a new era of socialism presided over by a leader who is easily the most far-left president since FDR, a man whose run for an Illinois Senate seat won the endorsement of the Illinois branch of Democratic Socialist of America and whose 2008 presidential campaign was celebrated by the Communist People's Weekly World.[2] Obama is aggressively expanding federal regulation of the economy on everything from financial management to electricity generation and personal energy use.

President Obama's administration does not follow the example and wisdom of our Founding Fathers but rather that of Karl Marx, who stated, "From each according to his abilities, to each according to his needs." He may have rephrased Marx in more acceptable language taken from the Bible, arguing that government has a duty to be our "brother's keeper" but the end he seeks is, ultimately, the same.

Obama's America is forcing fundamental change in America's economy that ultimately weakens and destroys the work of the Founding Fathers. Obama's policies will take us from a Constitution that provides for a small government, free markets, and individual rights and move us further toward one that empowers BIG government, controlled markets and collective rights. In Obama's United States, we will break free from the "constraints that were placed by the Founding Fathers in the Constitution" and accomplish "social justice" through "redistributive" change — all in pursuit of his "brother's keeper" model. This is the socialistic threat we face as Obama works to re-make America in his image.

2

The "I Believe in the Free Market" LIE

"Contrary to the claims of some of my critics, I am an ardent believer in the free market. I believe businesses like yours are the engines of economic growth in this country. You create the jobs." [3] —BHO

A year into his massive economic stimulus spending program, the Wall Street and Detroit bailouts, and on the cusp of his government takeover of American health care, Barack Obama came before the Business Roundtable on February 24, 2010, to tout his pro-business bona fides. Claiming to be an "ardent believer in the free market," and sounding much like Ronald Reagan, Obama told business leaders, "I firmly believe that America's success in large part depends on your success."

Obama later contradicted himself when he delivered a withering critique of the "same old tune" of market solutions, cutting regulations and reducing taxes as the way out of economic decline. In a December 6,

2011 speech, Obama derided those who say "The market will take care of everything," calling it a "simple theory" that "fits well on a bumper sticker." That theory "doesn't work," Obama said, updating his Business Roundtable speech.

With unemployment at 8.3 percent and the Gross Domestic Product (GDP) at just 3 percent after almost three years of his deficit spending solution, the President announced that the free market formula for economic growth "has never worked. It didn't work when it was tried in the decade before the Great Depression.... I mean, understand, it's not as if we haven't tried this theory."[4]

Actually, it's worked whenever it's been tried. America enjoyed sustained economic growth from 1922 to 1929 after Harding and Coolidge cut taxes and spending, and left business alone. Reagan did much the same and launched the longest period of sustained economic growth in U.S. history.[5]

3

The "I'm A Christian" DECEPTION

"I am a Christian." —BHO

Franklin Graham demonstrated in early 2012 just how dicey it is to challenge this central plank of Barack Obama's biography. He wound up apologizing to President Obama after hostile media reaction and a chorus of boo-bird black pastors protested his very public doubt about the President's claim to faith.

But challenge we must.

Here's why. Obama's revealing 2004 interview with journalist Kathleen Falsani[6] demonstrates a man at odds with core Christian beliefs. Case in point: Jesus asserted that He, alone, is the way to God. Or, as His follower Peter put it, "there is no other name [than Jesus] under heaven given among men by which we must be saved" (Acts 4:12 NKJV). That's standard-issue Christianity, but Barack begs to differ. "I believe that there are many paths to the same place," he told Falsani, citing a mix of "Eastern influences," Islam, and Judaism on his religious formation.

Sin, for him, is "being out of alignment with my values" (not God's), and he doesn't know what will happen to him after death. He hangs what hope he has for the hereafter on his own good deeds not what Christ did for him by dying on a cross. "What I believe in is that if I live my life as well as I can, that I will be rewarded." That may be what he learned in the church of his "good friend," Rev. Wright, but Christianity teaches the exact opposite: "For by grace you have been saved through faith, and that not of yourselves; it is the gift of God" (Eph. 2:8). Barack may say he's a believer, but not, it seems, in what the Bible teaches or what Christians have affirmed for nearly 2,000 years.

4

The "Brother's Keeper" LIE

"I am my brother's keeper..." —BHO

Barack Obama has been saying this for years, most recently at the 2012 National Prayer Breakfast where he argued that Jesus would support raising taxes on the rich. Our "theologian-in-chief" mixes up Marx with Jesus when he argues that a biblical command obligating individuals ("love your neighbor as yourself") applies to civic government and justifies the "coerced compassion" of redistributionist tax policy.

He also exposes himself as a rank hypocrite when one sees how little he has done for his own half-brother. When candidate Obama was citing the obligation to be our "brother's keeper" in 2008, brother George Hussein Obama was making do in a squalid Kenyan slum.[7] A visitor found George living in a "single room with a foul stench of stale cigarette and fresh pot smoke." George said he does not get any support from his millionaire older half-brother.

Barack Obama has also been on the stingy side when it comes to his own charitable giving. He gave less than 1 percent of the $1.2 million he and wife Michelle earned between 2000 and 2004[8] and just 6 percent in 2008,[9] when earnings grew to $2.7 million. His giving has since grown, rising to 14 percent in 2010.[10] That's respectable but his own half-brother George is still not among the charitable causes he supports. Barack is not his own (half) brother's keeper.

5

The "Collective Salvation" DECEPTION

"Our individual salvation always depends on our collective salvation."[11] —BHO

The "collective salvation" of which Obama has frequently spoken is not a Christian concept, but a Marxist one dressed up in its Sunday best and known as liberation theology. Black Liberation Theology sees all of life as a struggle of liberation from oppressors. It addresses the plight of blacks living in the "Egypt" of the United States seeking liberation from whites. Black liberation theology is focused on the community's struggle against oppressors, and regards salvation (liberation) coming through the community being set free.

Similarly, Obama's theology links individual and corporate salvation. His idea that "individual salvation depends on our collective salvation" is far afield from the traditional view of salvation explained by Jesus, interpreted by the apostles, and continued for 2,000 years by Christians of many denominations. Christianity does not make the individual's salvation dependent on anything "collective." Salvation is based on the finished work of Christ and the individual's response to Him. Earthly/political "salvation" will come only with Jesus' return.

But if salvation is a collective enterprise, as Obama believes, then politics becomes the vehicle for its achievement and that is a very dangerous undertaking. "Wherever politics tries to be redemptive it is promising too much," said Pope Benedict. "Where it wishes to do the work of God, it becomes not divine, but demonic." But that is what Mr. Obama, aided and abetted by friends on the Religious Left, is attempting to do. He seeks the "collective salvation" of society through wealth redistribution and the heavy hand of government over all of life, and all for the "collective good."

6

The "We're Not A Christian Nation" LIE

"We do not consider ourselves a Christian nation, or a Jewish nation, or a Muslim nation. We consider ourselves a nation of citizens who are bound by ideals and a set of values." [12] —BHO

This is factually false. Americans, by 62 percent, do consider ours to be a Christian nation, according to a 2009 Newsweek poll.[13] And some 78 percent of Americans claim to be Christian.[14] But despite these inconvenient facts, Obama is working to legitimize moral relativism and take our nation in another spiritual direction. He believes that the idea of America being a nation with a prevailing and dominant Judeo-Christian ethos is at best a thing of the past. Instead of society being joined together by an overarching belief in a Creator, the new orthodoxy says that all beliefs and ideas are equal and must be tolerated. The only thing that cannot be tolerated is dogmatism, especially religious dogmatism.

What does this mean for those living in a post-Christian nation under Obama's administration? The stripping of religious symbols such as crosses and the Ten Commandments barely scratches the surface. As the statist government stretches its tentacles deeper and deeper into every facet of the economy and society, Judeo-Christian beliefs are coming directly into conflict with the law, and our liberties are at risk. ObamaCare has created a vast, new front-line in the clash between statist government and religious values of which the fight over the ObamaCare contra-ceptives/sterilizations/abortion pill mandate is just one instance. Under Obama's vision of a post-Christian America, followers of Christ find themselves faced with a choice between upholding their faith or fulfilling a politically-correct government mandate.

7

The "My Church Is Normal" LIE

"I don't think my church is actually particularly controversial."[15] — BHO

Obama doesn't think his church is "particularly controversial." On the other hand, not too many congregations have pastors who denounce our nation as steeped in racism, call it the "U.S. of KKK A.," praise communist Cuba after traveling twice to the island nation in the 1980s, and blame the U.S. government for AIDS.

But it's not just Rev. Jeremiah Wright's fiery rhetoric, communist sympathy, and crackpot theories that set Trinity United Church apart. The church Mr. Obama attended for 20 years is singular in its devotion to Black Liberation Theology, teaching for example, that Jesus was black, and that America's white church is the "anti-Christ." That's not normal Sunday school fare in most churches, black or white, but under Rev. Wright, a disciple of black liberation theologian James Cone, Trinity has embraced a strange amalgamation of "old-time religion" and Marxist theory. Cone, author of *Black Theology and Black Power,* has written that "together, black religion and Marxist philosophy may show us the way to build a completely new society."

While black church leaders in America heavily lean Democratic, few African-American congregations embrace Cone's melding of Marx and Jesus. In that sense, says *Radical-in-Chief* author Stanley Kurtz, Trinity United is something of an "outlier." Cone told a reporter, "I would point to that church (Trinity) first," when asked which church in the U.S. best exemplifies his radical theology.[16] As Kurtz writes, "Obama arguably belonged to the most radical black church in the country."[17]

8

The Reverend Wright Denial LIE

"I have known Reverend Wright for almost 20 years....
[His comments] certainly don't portray accurately
my values and beliefs." [18] —BHO

President Obama faced one extremely high hurdle on his path to the presidency: Rev. Jeremiah Wright. Pastor, mentor and close friend to Obama, Wright's caustic, hate-filled diatribes provided most Americans with their first introduction to something called Black Liberation Theology. Statements like "Jesus was a black man" and "God damn America" sent shockwaves through the political discourse.

Obama survived political disaster by first stating that he was unaware of Wright's views and then later renouncing his church membership and association with Wright. But that was hardly the end of the story because the Obama-Wright relationship runs deep. Obama credits Wright for his Christian conversion. Wright baptized the Obama children, blessed their house and served as spiritual guide and mentor to Obama. Obama sat in Wright's congregation for 20 years listening to his sermons. What he heard was what fellow congregant Oprah Winfrey also heard. Wright's inflammatory angry pulpiteering was a major reason she left the church by the mid-1990s.[19] Not Obama. "Most of the time, when I'm in church," Obama said, "he's talking about Jesus, God, faith, values, caring for the poor...."

That, and other denials of his knowledge of Wright, "was deeply dishonest," says researcher Stanley Kurtz. He notes that the two men had an intellectual bond. As Wright told an Obama biographer, "We talked about race and politics." Obama was familiar with the incendiary views of Wright's intellectual mentor, black liberation theologian James Cone, and intentionally chose Wright's church, Trinity United Church of Christ "in full knowledge of Wright's radical theological views..." and "precisely *because* of those radical views."[20] It's no surprise Obama acted as he did to distance himself from Wright and deny any knowledge of his pastor's radical beliefs. Wright is a window into Obama's socialist past, something he had to hide at all costs in 2008 from the American public.

9

The "Deeply Disappointed" at Father Pfleger LIE

"I am deeply disappointed in Father Pfleger's divisive, backward-looking rhetoric."[21] — BHO

It fails the laugh test to believe that the angry oratory of Obama's long-time friend and ally, Father Michael Pfleger, disappointed Obama for any reason other than that it set back his campaign. Pfleger had stepped into the pulpit of Trinity United Church of Christ on May 25, 2008, to unleash a jeremiad against "white entitlement and supremacy," complete with mean-spirited mockery of Hillary Clinton. The crowd at Obama's home church laughed, cheered, and rose to their feet in approval.

Father Pfleger's shtick was well-known to them as it was to his friend, Barack, who has spoken in Pfleger's church and first met the radical priest some 20 years prior while working as a community organizer.[22] In 1987 community organizer Obama tapped Pfleger to serve on the advisory committee of his youth counseling initiative. And in 1992, Pfleger served, along with representatives from ACORN and SEIU Local 880, on the steering committee of Obama's Project Vote, a voter registration effort that helped elect Carol Moseley Braun to the U.S. Senate.[23] Obama researcher Stanley Kurtz reports that Obama, Pfleger, Rev. Wright, ACORN, and others "were all part of a single tightly interconnected political alliance."[24] Or as Obama told journalist Cathleen Falsani in 2004, "Father Michael Pfleger is a dear friend, and somebody I interact with closely."[25]

10

The Bill Ayers LIE

"This is a guy who lives in my neighborhood, who's a professor of English in Chicago who I know." —BHO

It was in the spacious Hyde Park home of unrepentant terrorists Bill Ayers and Bernadine Dohrn that Barack Obama's political coming-out party took place in 1995. That event, at which retiring Illinois state senator Alice Palmer tabbed Obama as her heir apparent, points to the connection Obama has with these '60s radicals who have both taken up respectable perches in academia. But that Ayers-hosted soiree for the young politician is just one of the links America's 44th president has with a man who was part of the violent Weather Underground, a group which bombed the U.S. Capitol, the Pentagon, and other government buildings. Looking back on those days, Ayers told the *New York Times* in 2001, "I don't regret setting bombs. I feel we didn't do enough."

More than just a Hyde Park neighbor, Obama has made common cause with Ayers in advancing mutually held radical goals. Ayes served with Obama for eight years on the boards of two leftist foundations. With Ayers' help, Obama became board chairman of the Chicago Annenberg Challenge where the future president joined Ayers and others in dishing out some $50 million to likeminded groups like ACORN and other community organizing groups. The two men served together on the Woods Fund of Chicago, giving grants to groups like the Midwest Academy, described by researcher Stanley Kurtz as "arguably the most influential institutional force in community organizing from the seventies through the nineties, and very much a crypto-socialist organization."[26] And Obama joined Ayers and Dohrn in fighting a common-sense measure favored by prosecutors to reform the Illinois juvenile justice system in 1997. Obama knows that Ayers, like Rev. Wright, is a window into his socialist roots and has pulled the blinds down tight.

11

The ACORN Denial LIE

---

*"The only involvement I've had with ACORN was
I represented them alongside the U.S. Justice
Department in making Illinois implement a
Motor Voter Law."*[27] —**BHO**

Candidate Obama dismissed questions about his
ties to ACORN, along with accusations that the
group engaged in voter fraud, calling such charges a
"distraction." His only link to ACORN (The
Association of Community Organizations for
Reform Now), he said, was litigating a Motor Voter
lawsuit on behalf of the community organization.
That was it. The Obama campaign fiercely
repudiated "naked lies about his supposed
connection to ACORN," asserting that "ACORN
was not part of Project Vote, the successful voter
registration drive Barack ran in 1992."[28]

But that's not what Barack told ACORN leaders in a
videotape that came to light in February 2010.
Speaking to ACORN officials in pursuit of the
group's endorsement of his presidential bid, Obama
touts his long and close ties to ACORN from Project
Vote up until his service in the U.S. Senate: "When I
ran Project Vote, voter registration drive in Illinois,
ACORN was smack dab in the middle of it. Once I
was elected, there wasn't a campaign that ACORN
worked on down in Springfield that I wasn't right
there with you. Since I've been in the United States
Senate, I've been always a partner with ACORN as
well. I've been fighting with ACORN, alongside
ACORN, on issues you care about, my entire career."[29]

The video came out after the election and Obama's dishonesty on ACORN spared his bid for the presidency. Had we known then what we know now about Obama's ties to this "classic socialist front group," as researcher Stanley Kurtz calls ACORN, Obama's campaign would have capsized and sunk.

12

The "Michelle's Patriotism" LIE

"What she meant was, this is the first time that she's been proud of the politics of America." [30] —BHO

Maybe Obama was just doing what any husband would do for his wife, if she said something shocking or scandalous. He'd try to cover for her, defend her, and, yes, stretch the truth in doing so. So give him points for at least trying to deny the obvious import of what wife Michelle said twice on February 18, 2008, telling crowds in Milwaukee and Madison, Wisconsin that, "for the first time in my adult lifetime, I am proud of my country, because it feels like hope is finally making a comeback." [31]

Somehow, at age 44, Mrs. Obama had never felt pride in a nation that enjoyed freedom and prosperity largely unknown in human history; won the Cold War; attracted legal immigrants from across the globe; led the world in science, technology, and the arts; and more.

So what was it that, at long last, caused pride to swell in her heart in 2008? She almost spelled it out two days later in her remarks in Milwaukee and Madison, telling a gathering in Rhode Island, "When was the last time you've seen a presidential candidate who could claim victories in states like Idaho and Missouri and Washington and Louisiana and Georgia and Maine and Hawaii. We haven't seen that before ... in a while."[32] Well, we do see presidential candidates win victories in the above states every four years. What we haven't seen is a black presidential candidate winning all those states. And that, while she didn't exactly say so, was what Mrs. Obama could finally feel pride in America about. At long last, the racist white America that so enraged Rev. Wright and many in his congregation was giving way to "hope and change."

13

The "Constitution is Evolving" DECEPTION

"[The Constitution] is not a static but rather a living document and must be read in the context of an ever-changing world."[33] —BHO

Since about 1950, American jurisprudence has taken a frightening turn. The Constitution has become a living document whose meaning depends on the "evolving standards" of society, not what the words actually state. Who determines what those "standards" are? Simply stated, all-powerful judges, who have become the arbiters and executors of our laws.

With the addition of Supreme Court justices Sonia Sotomayor and Elena Kagan, we are already seeing that Obama's courts will promote the liberal view of an "evolving" or "living" Constitution. Obama's Supreme Court will care more about the "change we need" than the Constitution we are to live by. That means a panoply of new rights are about to be discovered in the Constitution, including rights to welfare, affirmative action, government-financed abortions, homosexual marriage, assisted suicide, and human cloning. Add to that ending capital punishment, the wholesale release of criminal defendants, approval for draconian damage awards against legitimate business, and "bans" on educational vouchers for religious schools and religious symbols on public buildings and our currency.

"Change has come to America," Obama announced on Election night. What he failed to say is that much of the change will be implemented without the people or their representatives ever casting a vote by his appointed judges who, like him, treat the Constitution like putty to be shaped as they wish.

Section Two
Campaign Lies

To win the White House, Barack Obama had to not only shed his unsavory past, ala Wright, Pfleger, Ayers, and ACORN, he also had to transform himself into a favor factory, doling out promises left and right—well, mostly left—in order to generate thrills up the legs of voters (and his friends in the media) nationwide. He issued a raft of "good government" pledges: post-partisanship, transparency, a lobbyist-free White House, earmark reform, whistleblower protection, and more. But that was then, this is now. Here are a few of the broken promises now littering his campaign trail.

14

The "Most Transparent in History" LIE

"My Administration is committed to creating an unprecedented level of openness in Government. We will work together to ensure the public trust and establish a system of transparency, public partici-pation, and collaboration."[34] —**BHO**

The White House bragged on Inauguration Day that the Obama administration would be "the most open and transparent in history." Instead, advocates of open government now suggest his may be the least transparent. A Washington attorney who has worked with six administrations since 1978 in filing Freedom of Information Act (FOIA) requests told Politico, "It's kind of shocking to me to say this, but of the six, this administration is the worst on FOIA issues. The worst. There's just no question about it.... This administration is raising one barrier after another. ... It's gotten to the point where I'm stunned — I'm really stunned."[35]

Politico reports that the White House has prosecuted whistle-blowers, fought FOIA requests in court, "sometimes on Obama's direct orders," and advocated less openness in government before the U.S. Supreme Court. Assistant Solicitor General Anthony Yang disagreed when Justice Sonia Sotomayor said the FOIA law should promote "full disclosure" and that exceptions to it should be narrowly drawn in order to promote transparency. When Justice Antonin Scalia asked Yang if the Obama administration "wants to abandon the principle ... that exceptions to FOIA are to be narrowly construed," Yang answered, "We do not embrace that principle."[36]

David Sobel, senior counsel at the Electronic Frontier Foundation, calls it "just incredible for an administration that says it's committed to an unprecedented level of transparency to be telling the Supreme Court, 'Hey, we don't accept long-established Supreme Court precedent favoring disclosure.' It's just jaw-dropping."

15

The "Five-Day Public Review" LIE

"When there's a bill that winds up on my desk you the public will have five days to find out what's in it before I sign it, so that you know what your government's doing." [37]—BHO

Crowds cheered candidate Obama when he made this popular pledge. But once in office, he made it the first to be broken, violating his sunlight before signing commitment in just nine days. Only six of the 124 bills Obama signed into law in his first year in office were posted on the White House website for a five-day review and comment period. One of those bills, the American Recovery Act, was kept out of public view before passage while Democrats worked behind closed doors to write it. They approved it without any Republican support and sent it to the President who signed it one day after it was presented to him. A five-day public review probably wouldn't have changed the outcome, but it would have given Americans the chance at least to discover some of the last-minute add-ons in the bill like an amendment giving AIG executives a honey-pot of bonuses worth millions.[38] The Cato Institute's Jim Harper reports that after three years, just 247 of the 478 bills signed by the President were put up on the White House website for a five-day review. That, sports fans, is a sunlight before signing record of just 52.4 percent.

16

The "No Lobbyists in the White House" DECEPTION

"If you are a lobbyist entering my administration, you will not be able to work on matters you lobbied on, or in the agencies you lobbied during the previous two years." [39] —BHO

Obama made good, it seemed, on this campaign promise to keep lobbyists from running the White House when he signed an executive order on his first day in office to restrict the hiring of former lobbyists. But he quickly bent the rule by issuing waivers to bring on those he formerly derided as "influence peddlers." Lobbyists winning waivers to pass through the government-industry revolving door include former Raytheon lobbyist William J. Lynn to be Deputy Defense Secretary; Jocelyn Frye, former lobbyist for National Partnership for Women and Families, hired as Director of Policy and Projects in the Office of the First Lady; and Cecilia Munoz, a former lobbyist for the National Council of La Raza, who came on as Director of Intergovernmental Affairs in the Executive Office of the President in 2009 and now presides as head of the President's Domestic Policy Council.

Despite these lobbyists, and others, Obama touted his anti-lobbying bona fides in his 2010 State of the Union speech, claiming that "we've excluded lobbyists from policy-making jobs." Not so. In fact, the White House hired a high-profile lobbyist in March 2012 to serve as a counselor to Vice President Biden. PolitiFact, which is tracking some 513 Obama promises, rates this Obama pledge a "Promise Broken."[40]

17

The "Health Care Talks On C-SPAN" LIE

"We'll have the [health care reform] negotiations televised on C-SPAN, so that people can see who is making arguments on behalf of their constituents, and who are making arguments on behalf of drug companies and insurance companies." [41] —BHO

Despite Obama's oft-repeated campaign promise to conduct negotiations for his health care overhaul in the public eye, ObamaCare was crafted largely behind closed doors. Obama's promise of C-SPAN coverage of negotiations never took place, even though C-SPAN president Brian Lamb sent a letter to congressional leaders asking them to open "all important negotiations, including any conference committee meetings, to electronic media coverage"[42]

Asked why no sunshine was allowed into health care deliberations, White House spokesman Robert Gibbs said, "I don't think the President intimated that every decision putting together a health care bill would be on public TV."[43] Maybe he wasn't in the audience on January 31, 2008, when Obama said in a debate, "That's what I will do in bringing all parties together, not negotiating behind closed doors, but bringing all parties together, and broadcasting those negotiations on C-SPAN so that the American people can see what the choices are...."

Private, not public, discussions were the rule as ObamaCare legislation moved forward. McClatchey reported in July 2009 that "the two biggest deals so far — industry agreements to cut drug and hospital costs — were reached in secret."[44] Senate Finance Committee chairman Max Baucus confirmed that the deal struck with the pharmaceutical industry to lower drug costs for seniors was reached after private talks, and a pharmaceutical industry official said those private talks that had the White House's "blessing." In another instance, Vice President Joe Biden stood with hospital executives at a press event announcing a deal reached in private to cut $155 billion from government programs. They refused to take questions.

18

The "Earmark Reform" DECEPTION

"Absolutely, we need earmark reform. And when I'm president, I will go line by line to make sure that we are not spending money unwisely."[45] —BHO

Candidate Obama pledged to return "earmarks to less than $7.8 billion a year, the level they were at before 1994"[46] President Obama didn't even come close. Taxpayers for Common Sense says that Obama approved some 9,499 earmarks costing $15.9 billion in fiscal year 2010.[47] And Republicans contend that the $787 billion stimulus bill Obama signed into law contained numerous earmarks including, said Wyoming GOP Senator Mike Enzi, $850 million for Amtrak, $75 million for the Smithsonian, and $1 billion for the 2010 census.[48]

Since then, Mr. Obama has joined with Republicans in calling for an end to earmarks, something he couldn't achieve when Democrats ran Congress. And aside from ending earmarks, the credibility of Mr. Obama's commitment to "not spending money unwisely" is shredded by the fact that three years into his presidency federal debt has shot up by almost $5 trillion. Instead of going line by line through spending bills, Mr. Obama's well-rehearsed solution to America's chronic fiscal red ink is not to cut spending but, always, hike taxes on the "rich."

19

The "I'm Listening" DECEPTION

"I will listen to you, especially when we disagree."[49]
—BHO

Instead of listening, Barack Obama wants to use the power of the Executive branch to silence conservative opposition and deliver a damaging blow to free speech for all Americans. Throughout his campaign and now his presidency he has demonized, demeaned, and bullied conservative media such as Fox News, Rush Limbaugh and Sean Hannity.

The effort to "Hush Rush" and other conservative talkers got a boost early in Obama's term when congressional Democrats talked up a return to the Fairness Doctrine — a policy that requires broadcast media to promote "fairness" and "balance." Removed by Ronald Reagan in 1987, the Fairness Doctrine would silence conservatives, especially in talk radio. That effort failed but Mr. Obama is also a strong supporter of "Net Neutrality," which would essentially create a Fairness Doctrine for the Internet.

It would censor every American's actions on the Internet – all in the name of "fairness".

And in 2010 Obama's Federal Trade Commission published a 47-page statist plan for the "Reinvention of Journalism." This document represents what may be an unprecedented attempt by the federal government to control and directly fund liberal-biased journalism. The FTC proposal includes a funding increase for public radio and television, a $4 billion yearly tax on consumer electronics, and a so-called "Drudge Tax" that targets websites such as the Drudge Report. Instead of "listening," the Obama administration is working to control the free flow of information while imposing punitive taxes on political opponents and censoring and stifling critical media.

20

The "No Super PAC Money" LIE

"For what we are facing is no less than a potential corporate takeover of our elections. And what is at stake is no less than the integrity of our democracy." [50] —BHO

Obama chastised members of the U.S. Supreme Court in 2010 for lifting a congressional ban on corporate political expenditures and resorted to purple prose in decrying the decision, saying in a radio address that "the integrity of our democracy" was at stake. Two years later, Obama has decided it's not such a bad idea after all to open the "floodgates for special interests" as he once put it. Up until February 6, 2012, Obama spoke out often and forcefully against the corrupting influence of big money in politics. The president warned that "all across America, special interests have poured millions of dollars into phony front groups," and urged against "a corporate takeover of our democracy...."[51]

But then he changed his mind, inviting donors, through his campaign chairman, to give to a White House-favored Super PAC. Super PACs are political campaign committees allowed to make expenditures in support or opposition to candidates for office and to which corporations, unions, and individuals may make unlimited contributions.

The about face came, campaign chairman Jim Messina argued, because the Obama campaign could not afford to "unilaterally disarm" in the race for cash. The reversal was similar to another by Obama in 2008 when he changed his mind and withdrew from the federal campaign finance system. The change came after Obama recognized his fund-raising prowess would dramatically outstrip the funds available to spend if he took the federal dollars. Force to choose between his "principles" and his election, Obama made the easy choice.

21

The "Post-Partisan" LIE

"Then you've got [the GOP's] plan, which is, let's have dirtier air, dirtier water, less people with health insurance." [52] —BHO

Obama's grotesque charge against his Republican

opponents is so over the top that it could belong in a comedy routine. It sounds much like a *Saturday Night Live* satire of a Bush/Gore debate in which the Al Gore character says, "Under my plan, Etta's prescription drugs would be covered. Under my opponent's plan, her house would be burned to the ground."[53] Of course, Obama was serious and no one laughed when the President (who is largely off limits to TV comedy-writers) offered an equally outrageous distortion of his opponents at a campaign stop in Asheville, North Carolina.

Obama's slam on Republicans contradicts his Inaugural Address call for "an end to the petty grievances and false promises, the recriminations and worn-out dogmas that for far too long have strangled our politics."[54] It's a theme he has long sounded in his effort to cast himself as a "post-partisan" leader. Obama told the 2004 Democratic convention that "There is not a liberal America and a conservative America; there is the United States of America!" The truth, says *New Yorker* magazine writer Ryan Lizza, is that "Obama's actual political biography is more partisan and ruthless than the version he has told over the years in countless 'post-partisan' speeches...."[55]

And despite the President's cheap words, what the GOP and those who love liberty really want is not dirty air and water, but an end to burdensome environmental regulations that destroy jobs, stall economic growth, harm those at the bottom of the economic ladder, and expand Washington's control over our lives.

22

The "Protection for Whistleblowers" LIE

"Barack Obama will strengthen whistleblower laws to protect federal workers who expose waste, fraud, and abuse of authority in government." [56]— BHO

Consider this a promise broken. The Obama White House fired a federal inspector who investigated Obama's friend and Sacramento Mayor Kevin Johnson and then offered a series of false reasons for the termination. In 2008, inspector Gerald Walpin investigated St. HOPE, a California nonprofit run by Johnson, a former NBA star, and found it had mishandled an $850,000 AmeriCorps grant. Walpin's finding led to the suspension of St. Hope and Johnson from future federal grants.

That became a problem after Johnson won election as Sacramento mayor in November 2008. His suspension raised the possibility that Sacramento would be ineligible for stimulus monies. Political pressure mounted on Walpin to agree to lift the suspension, but he refused, and that's when the White House stepped in to fire the inspector. The White House justified his firing by citing behavioral concerns, claiming that Walpin was "confused, disoriented, unable to answer questions" and that he "exhibited a lack of candor ... to decision makers." But no facts supported those charges.

When Iowa Senator Charles Grassley looked into the firing, the White House stonewalled his inquiry, providing "incomplete and misleading" information. After much digging, Grassley and Rep. Darrell Issa produced a congressional report that cleared Walpin and suggested that the White House had "orchestrated an after-the-fact smear campaign to justify" Walpin's firing. [57]

Politically motivated firing, stonewalling, and a smear campaign. Not what we'd expect from a White House pledged to protect "federal workers who expose waste, fraud, and abuse."

Section Three
Big Government Lies

"I'm from the government and I'm here to help." Obama never used those words, tagged by Ronald Reagan as "the nine most terrifying words in the English language." He's just lived them. For him, government is the solution (unlike Reagan who said government is the problem). But his great expectations for Big Government solutions have not worked out so well. The stimulus, bailouts, government job creation efforts, not to mention the misbegotten "Cash for Clunkers" plan, have all showcased the sizeable gap between his rhetoric and our reality. Herewith we chronicle some of the Obama Big Government Lies.

23

The "Create Or Save Jobs" LIE

The stimulus law will "create or save" 3.5 million jobs, and "a new wave of innovation, activity and construction will be unleashed across America" that will bring "real and lasting change for generations to come."[58] —BHO

He didn't quite say it was the "moment when the rise of the oceans began to slow and the planet began to heal" but expectations were still very high for Obama's February 2009 stimulus law. Let's take a quick look at what has come of Obama's grand expectations for his rushed-into-law stimulus.

The President's economic advisers said unemployment, which was 6.8 percent in the month he was elected and 7.6 percent in January 2009, would stay below 8 percent as a result of pumping more than $787 billion into the economy. To the contrary, unemployment rose dramatically after the stimulus was passed, reaching 9.9 percent in May 2010. The official unemployment figure for January 2012 was still 8.3 percent, showing no improvement after three years of alleged stimulus. But that official stat understates the true picture. Real unemployment, which counts unemployment, under employment, and people who have given up the active search for work, was 15.1 percent in January 2012, according to the Bureau of Labor Statistics.[59]

That's not all. The ranks of the long-term unemployed — workers unable to find a job for more than 27 months — have grown 83 percent in the last three years to 5.5 million people. The number of civilian workers has declined by 126,000 and labor force participation, a measure of the number of adults employed or seeking employment, has dropped three percent—not what you'd expect to see in an economic recovery. Finally, median annual household income is down seven percent from where it stood in February 2009.[60]

To recap, unemployment is unchanged, the number of long-term jobless has ballooned, and households have less money to spend. This is what "real and lasting change for generations to come" looks like— unless, of course, real change of another sort comes in November.

24

The "Stimulus Law is Working" LIE

*"We began by passing a Recovery Act that has already
saved or created over 150,000 jobs."* [61] —BHO

President Obama signed the "Recovery Act" into
law on February 28, 2009. In the following two
months, some 1.2 million more workers took home
pink slips rather than checks. So where did Mr.
Obama come up with the alleged 150,000 jobs
"saved or created" by the Recovery Act within his
first 100 days in office? From an estimate furnished
by his own Council of Economic Advisers, not hard
data from the job market. Factcheck.org took a look
at Obama's new employment math and concluded:
"The President's claim is really an estimate of what
his economic advisers think the stimulus bill is doing,
and not based on any evidence of its actual effects."[62]

But now that the $831 billion stimulus "pig" has
made its way through America's economic python,
what's left? Not much. The Congressional Budget
Office estimated in February 2012 that stimulus
spending added between 300,000 and 2 million jobs.
That's quite a range and might be impressive except
for one glaringly obvious fact. The economy actually
had 400,000 fewer employed workers in January
2012 than 3 years earlier when Congress rushed to
pass the massive spending measure. And two
economists have argued that the Recovery Act has
actually made things worse. They estimated that
stimulus spending "created/saved approximately
450,000 state and local government jobs and
destroyed/forestalled roughly one million private

sector jobs...." Had tax dollars not been dumped into state and local municipalities, "many government workers (on average relatively well-educated) would have found private-sector employment had their jobs not been saved." [63]

25

The "I'll Cut The Deficit" LIE

"That's why today I'm pledging to cut the deficit we inherited by half by the end of my first term in office." [64] —BHO

President Obama will have to bring the deficit down to $650 billion by Nov. 2012 in order to make good on the promise he made to the nation barely a month into his term. He won't even come close. Instead of making hard choices to cut spending, Obama's budgets have busted any sense of fiscal responsibility. The official on-budget deficit for Obama's first three years (excluding funds stolen from the Social Security Trust Fund totaled: $1.55 Trillion (2009), $1.37 Trillion (2010) and $1.36 Trillion (2009) — each of which more than doubled the highest prior budget deficit in history.[65] Obama's fiscal 2013 budget includes a deficit of $901 billion. The Congressional Budget Office projects that the actual deficit will be closer to $1 trillion.[66]

It's hard to believe Obama was serious when he issued his 2009 pledge, sternly announcing, "I refuse to leave our children with a debt that they cannot repay and that means taking responsibility right now, in this administration for getting our spending under control." Those are words every Tea Party patriot could embrace, but what followed was a spending spree of historic proportions. Federal debt exploded by more than $4 trillion in Obama's first 1,000 days in office—adding as much debt as the U.S. accumulated from 1776 to 1993.[67] Total U.S. debt is now $15.4 trillion with nothing but red ink ahead.

26

The "Shovel-Ready Jobs" LIE

"We've got shovel-ready projects all across the country that governors and mayors are pleading to fund. And the minute we can get those investments to the state level, jobs are going to be created." [68]—BHO

President–elect Obama exuded confidence in December 2008 that his proposed stimulus bill would spark job creation throughout America. He knew, he said, that so-called "shovel ready" projects were lined up in the states, ready to start work once the flow of federal dollars started from Washington. At the signing ceremony for the "Recovery Act," Obama promised 400,000 new jobs from the stimulus investment in our nation's infrastructure alone. Two weeks later, he said "we are seeing shovels hit the ground."

The jobs didn't materialize, according to an Associated Press analysis which found ten months into the stimulus that "a surge in spending on roads and bridges has had no effect on local unemployment and only barely helped the beleaguered construction industry."[69] And what about those shovel-ready projects? Obama confessed to the *New York Times* in October 2010 that "there's no such thing as shovel-ready projects" when it comes to public works.[70] That was not something it took Mr. Obama a year and a half to learn. *New York Times* columnist David Brooks says Obama told him the same thing, off the record, a year earlier.[71]

The dubious prospect for jobs from massive infrastructure spending was known even before Obama took office. Author Ron Suskind writes that "Much of the infrastructure spending, meanwhile, was destined to languish unused, as it was made clear, even during the transition, that there were limits to how quickly money could be spent."[72]

27

The GM "Taxpayers Will Be Repaid" LIE

"American taxpayers are now positioned to recover more than my administration invested in GM, and that's a good thing."[73] —**BHO**

Obama celebrated General Motors' (GM) return to the stock market on November 18, 2010, boasting that taxpayers would be made whole on at least his part of the $50 billion bailout to GM. Don't count on it. Five months later, Obama Treasury Secretary Tim Geithner offered a more candid assessment: "We're going to lose money in the auto industry on net, but we did this for the jobs we were going to save, not to maximize return."[74]

That's not too reassuring to taxpayers who may be

out $14 billion on the GM bailout alone, given the steep slide in GM's stock price since January 2011. The stock has been declining since January 2011 and closed at $25.17 on March 23, 2012. That's less than half of the $53 per share needed to reimburse taxpayers for the funds dumped into GM (and United Auto Workers) coffers by the Bush and Obama administrations. As the GM stock tanks, the total projected taxpayer loss from the bailout has ballooned to $23.77 billion, according to a January 2012 Treasury estimate.[75]

Despite the bath taxpayers are taking on the bailout, Obama told a UAW convention on February 28, 2012 that the bailout "is paying off, not just for you but for America."[76] That's half right. Taxpayers are out billions, but the UAW and its members have done very well. The White House structured GM's bankruptcy, giving 17.5 percent of the new GM to the UAW pension fund and leaving UAW wages and pensions untouched. Meanwhile, old GM stockholders were wiped out.[77]

28

The "Business Will Be Hiring" DECEPTION

"Yesterday, Jim, the head of Caterpillar, said that if Congress passes our plan this company will be able to rehire some of the folks who were just laid off."[78] —BHO

Sometimes you just have to laugh. Obama was in

Peoria, Ohio, at a Caterpillar plant on February 14, 2009, to stump for his stimulus plan then in Congress. Standing in front of a huge Caterpillar rig, Obama announced "It is time for Congress to act..." to pass his bill. When they do, he said, "I believe it will be a major step forward on our path to economic recovery."

"And I'm not the only one who thinks so," Obama said, reading from his teleprompter. "Yesterday, Jim, the head of Caterpillar, said that if Congress passes our plan this company will be able to rehire some of the folks who were just laid off, and that's a story I'm confident will be repeated in companies across the country."[79]

Asked later if Caterpillar would in fact start rehiring if the stimulus passed Congress, "Jim," James Owens, then CEO and Board Chairman at Caterpillar, responded with reluctant candor: "I think, realistically no. I mean, the honest reality is we'll probably have to have more layoffs before we start hiring again." So, more layoffs ahead regardless of whether or not the stimulus bill passed. That was the story repeated not just at Caterpillar but in companies across the country as the stimulus passed and unemployment soared to 10 percent by October.

29

The "Cash for Clunkers" DECEPTION

Cash for Clunkers "has been successful beyond anybody's imagination." [80] —BHO

Back in 2009 when auto sales were down 34 percent from 2008, the auto industry and the UAW won Obama's support for a short-term auto industry stimulus program dubbed "Cash for Clunkers." The idea was to give consumers up to $4,500 of taxpayer dollars if they purchased new fuel-efficient cars and traded in their used cars which were destroyed.

Consumers flocked to auto showrooms to get their free money. Some 690,000 vehicles were sold in the short-lived program that cost nearly $3 billion and had to be canceled two months early. So what good did it do? None, according to a 2010 study which said consumers merely advanced car purchases they would have made anyway. The program "had no long run effect on auto purchases," according to the study.[81]

While 360,000 additional cars drove off lots in July and August of 2009, "in the seven months that followed, sales were down by 360,000 compared to what they would have been without the program,"[82] according to an NPR report on the study. The two economists who did the study said Cash for Clunkers provided no benefit to "employment, house prices, or household default rates in cities with higher exposure to the program."[83]

So no more cars were purchased and no jobs created — all for almost $3 billion. Well, there was one result of note. With so many used cars destroyed, inventory was reduced and the price of used cars rose 10 percent.[84] As Obama said, it's almost beyond imagination.

30

The "Chrysler Bailout" LIE

"Chrysler has repaid every dime and more of what it owes the American taxpayer from the investment we made during my watch." [85] —BHO

Mr. Obama made his triumphal claim that "Chrysler has repaid every dime and more" at a Toledo, Ohio, Chrysler plant on June 3, 2011. It's not true, as both the Associated Press [86] and Factcheck.org [87] have reported. American taxpayers are still missing — and will never see — $1.3 billion of the $12.5 billion in bailout money given to Chrysler under Bush and Obama. That's because the Obama administration forgave $1.6 billion of Chrysler's debt to taxpayers after the company declared bankruptcy.

Here's what happened. Chrysler got $4 billion from the government on Jan. 2, 2009 and another $8.5 billion on April 30, 2009, the same day it filed for bankruptcy. Chrysler Group LLC made its final repayment to the government on May 24, 2011, bringing its total payback to $10.6 billion. The U.S. Treasury Department acknowledged that same day that "Treasury is unlikely to fully recover its remaining outstanding investment of $1.9 billion in Chrysler." And why was that? Well, as a May 10, 2011 Government Accountability Office (GAO) report explained, the Obama administration Treasury Department "wrote off $1.6 billion from its loan to Chrysler." [88] A later sale of remaining government-owned Chrysler stock to Fiat netted the government about $560 million, leaving we, the taxpayers, still short $1.3 billion of the money given to Chrysler.

31

The "Stimulus Plan Fights Poverty" DECEPTION

The stimulus spending law is "a plan that rewards responsibility, lifting two million Americans from poverty by ensuring that anyone who works hard does not have to raise a child below the poverty line."[89] —BHO

Despite the President's promise, poverty in America has only increased since he signed the American Recovery and Reinvestment Act into law on February 17, 2009. Almost 10 million more Americans have entered the ranks of the poor since the 2007-2009 recession began, according to an Indiana University study released in January 2012. And more children are in poverty three years after the stimulus was passed as well, according to the Brookings Institution which predicts that, once data are in, the child poverty rate will have grown to 22 percent for 2011—up from 17.8 percent in 2007.[90]

The IU study found that the number of Americans living in poverty reached 46.2 million in 2010, a jump of 27 percent since 2006. The study, based on 2010 U.S. Census Bureau data, predicted that poverty would invade the lives of even more people in 2011 due to a stalled economy, high unemployment, and long-term unemployment.[91] All of which Mr. Obama confidently predicted would be tamed by the gusher of spending uncorked by his "stimulus."

32

The "Rich Pay Less In Taxes" LIE

"Middle-class families shouldn't pay higher taxes than millionaires and billionaires. That's pretty straight-forward. It's hard to argue against it." [92] —BHO

Actually, middle-class families don't pay higher taxes than millionaires and billionaires. The wealthy already pay more taxes, much more, as media fact checkers made clear after Obama invoked envy and the rhetoric of class warfare in a September 2011 Rose Garden pitch to hike taxes by $1.5 trillion.

Here are some facts. People earning more than $1 million in 2011 will pay 29.1 percent in federal taxes, according to the Tax Policy Center. The federal tax burden on middle-class earners, those making between $50,000 and $75,000, is half that at 15 percent.[93] Some 46 percent of all households, mainly those in the lower and middle income range, will pay no taxes for 2011. The wealthy, by contrast, shoulder a much greater share of the total tax burden. While the bottom 80 percent of wage earners contributed 10.9 percent to total federal tax revenue in 2010, the top .1 percent, people making more than $1.974 million, chipped in 16.4 percent of Uncle Sam's total tax take. And, as Jeffrey H. Anderson wrote in the *Weekly Standard*, "That's despite the fact that the bottom 80 percent collectively made more than six times as much money as the top 0.1 percent did."[94] The rich are already paying their "fair share," and then some.

33

The "No Middle-Class Tax Hike" LIE

"I can make a firm pledge. Under my plan, no family making less than $250,000 a year will see any form of tax increase." [95] —BHO

For Obama, taxes are not a necessary evil but a moral imperative. So when it comes to his radical social agenda, he's not about to let the middle class off the hook whatever he may have said to woo and win voters in 2008. Within his first 15 months in office, he signed into law at least 14 separate tax increases that target taxpayers earning less than $250,000 per year. [96]

Mr. Obama's tax pledge went up in smoke on, appropriately enough, April 1, 2009, when the federal bite on cigarette sales went up 156 percent, or some 61 cents a pack. [97] This hurts low-income Americans since, as Americans for Tax Reform reports, 25 percent of all smokers are under the poverty line and 55 percent of smokers belong to the "working poor." A year later, the President signed his signature legislative achievement, ObamaCare, into law and laid a new $503 billion tax increase on the backs of American workers, including those making less than $250,000 a year. [98] ObamaCare levies 18 new taxes including the universal mandate forcing individuals to buy health insurance. [99]

34

"Mortgage Bailout" DECEPTION

---

*"And through this [housing] plan, we will help
between 7 and 9 million families restructure or
refinance their mortgages so they can afford—avoid
foreclosure."*[100]

No wonder Tea Party "founder" Rick Santelli was
outraged. President Obama's mortgage bailout
program gave taxpayer dollars to unwise and
underwater homeowners, along with mortgage firms
who agreed to rewrite loans. "This is America!" he
thundered from the floor of the Chicago Board of
Trade on February 19, 2009. "How many of you
people want to pay for your neighbors' mortgage
that has an extra bathroom and can't pay their bills?"

That was the idea behind the President's Home
Affordable Refinance Program, launched in 2009
with the promise of aiding up to nine million
homeowners to reduce their monthly mortgages
and save their homes. The program gave loan
modification firms up to $3,500, including a dollar-
for-dollar match of part of the lender's costs, and
chipped in up to $5,000 to help homeowners pay
down their outstanding loan balance.[101]

The program has helped less than 2 million people
largely because it was limited to those with a loan-
to-value ratio of less than 125 percent, a rarity as
home values tumbled since 2009. The upside,
however, was that the program had cost taxpayers
some $2.5 billion, much less than the $50 billion
projected by Obama.[102] That, unfortunately, may

change now that the Obama administration has lifted the 125 percent LTV limitation in its revised 2012 version of his mortgage assistance program.[103] Doing so expands the "moral hazard" posed by the program and opens the door to transferring more taxpayer dollars to homeowners who want others to help pay for their mistakes.

Section Four
Domestic Policy Lies

Maybe he thinks we Americans are just fools. How else to explain the chutzpah Obama routinely demonstrates when making outrageous claims that can so easily be shown false. Like the time he told an audience in El Paso, Texas that the border fence is complete. Or his "happy days are here" claim that new auto fuel efficiency standards will save American families up to $8,000 a year in fill-up costs. "You like that?" Obama remarked when the crowd cheered. Flashing a broad grin, he added, "$8,000. That's no joke." Well, actually it is, but it's on us unless this joker is shuffled out of Washington next November. More lies, damned lies, and ObamaLies.

35

The "Border Fence Is Complete" LIE

"They wanted a [border] fence. Well, that fence is now basically complete."[104] —BHO

When President Obama said this in El Paso on May 10, 2011, just 36.3 miles, a mere five percent of the 700-mile double-layer fence Congress approved in 2006, had been built. And just 4.3 miles of the double-layer security barrier had been built since President Obama took office. Obama dislikes the "message" of the border fence, so much that he successfully halted work on the physical and virtual border fence. Despite committing to sending 1,200 unarmed National Guard troops to the U.S./Mexico border to help with intelligence and reconnaissance, he flatly refuses to take the necessary steps to protect our sovereignty and security — choosing instead to ridicule and threaten those who do and politicizing the immigration crisis to propel his push for comprehensive immigration reform (read: Amnesty).

For Obama, it's not about border security or national sovereignty — the immigration debate is about re-making America into his globalist view. Despite lack of progress on the double-layer fence, President Obama will continue to minimize government efforts to secure our borders while exposing our nation to more illegal, criminal and terrorist crossings at our borders.

36

The "Arizona Border Law Equals Discrimination" LIE

"Now suddenly if you don't have your papers and you took your kid out to get ice cream, you can be harassed. That's something that could potentially happen."[105] —BHO

With Arizona's border insecurities reaching a critical state, Arizona Governor Jan Brewer won passage of SB1070, a measure that takes over where the federal government had failed. The new law merely mimics the federal law — empowering state law enforcement to arrest illegal immigrants. Passage of the new law touched off a tumult of protest – and Mr. Obama led the way, claiming that "if you don't have your papers and you took your kid out to get ice cream, you can be harassed. That's something that could potentially happen."

Far from it! The law allows police to ask about immigration status only if there is reason to suspect a crime has been committed. But Obama has not let facts interrupt his opposition to border security. He sided with Mexico's President Felipe Calderon when he visited the White House and publicly condemned SB1070, saying "Such laws as the Arizona law ... is forcing our people to face discrimination." Standing shoulder-to-shoulder with Calderon, Obama rebuked Arizona for standing up for safe and secure borders, adding that "in the 21st Century we are not defined by our borders." It's obvious that Obama isn't interested in securing our borders, or even having those who come to the U.S. assimilate into our culture. No. In Obama's America he tells us, "Instead of worrying about whether immigrants can learn English ... you need to make sure that your child can speak Spanish."[106]

37

The "No Money for Illegal Immigrants" LIE

"There are also those who claim that our [health care] reform efforts would insure illegal immigrants. This,

too, is false. [107] —BHO

Rep. Joe Wilson shouted "You lie!" when Obama claimed in a speech to Congress that no ObamaCare funds would go to illegal immigrants. The House of Representatives rebuked Wilson for his outburst but now we learn he was right.

Health and Human Services handed out $28.8 million to 67 community health centers in August 2011, with $8.5 million going to "25 New Access Point awardees to target services to migrant and seasonal farm workers," according to Health Resources and Services Administration (HRSA) spokeswoman Judy Andrews. [108]

Andrews told CNSNews.com that the health centers are obligated under the ObamaCare grant to treat "all residents" who come in for treatment. "The Program's authorizing statute does not affirmatively address immigration status," said Andrews. "Rather, it simply states that health centers are required to provide primary health care to all residents of the health center's service area without regard for ability to pay." Since 25 percent of migrant workers are illegal immigrants, according to Pew Research, and the health centers are funded to target "migrant and seasonal farm workers," illegal immigrants will be receiving treatment under ObamaCare—just as Joe Wilson said.

38

"Fast And Furious" American Gun LIE

"90 percent of the guns recovered in Mexico come from the United States." [109] —BHO

In the midst of his global apology tour, Obama made a stop in Mexico and announced there on April 16, 2009, that the U.S. must share blame for the brutal Mexican drug war. After all, he said, "This war is being waged with guns purchased not here but in the United States." The President claimed that "more than 90 percent of the guns recovered in Mexico come from the United States."

It's too bad the President doesn't watch Fox News. Two weeks before his remarks in Mexico, Fox debunked the 90 percent number, using Bureau of Alcohol, Tobacco, and Firearms (ATF) statistics to show that just 17 percent of the guns found at Mexican crime scenes come from the U.S. [110]

So why did the President, along with Secretary of State Hillary Clinton, and even a top ATF official cite this grossly exaggerated 90 percent number? To make the case for stiffer gun control laws, say Second Amendment advocates. Weakening gun rights is also behind the government's secret "Fast and Furious" gun-running program in which thousands of U.S. purchased weapons were sent over the border into the hands of criminals in Mexico. It was an operation to be used, as internal ATF documents show, to press for a new rule on gun sales. [111] The killing of one federal agent [112] and 200 murders in Mexico [113] are linked to the Fast and Furious program. Plenty of reason for outrage there—and for congressional inquiry into this bizarre scheme.

39

The "Gradual Adjustment" of Gas Prices LIE

"I think that I would have preferred a gradual adjustment." [114] —BHO

With gas prices climbing, a reporter asked Obama on March 6, 2012, whether he wants the cost of fuel to go even higher in order to wean Americans off their dependence on oil. "Just from a political perspective, do you think a president of the United States going into reelection wants gas prices to go up higher?" [115] Obama asked. The answer seems obvious, but on June 10, 2008, when gas had hit $4 a gallon, another reporter posed the same question to then-candidate Obama. His answer was much more revealing.

In an interview with CNBC's John Harwood, Obama stressed the need to "adopt renewable, clean energies like solar, wind and biodiesel," leading Harwood to ask if high gas prices would provide an "incentive so that we do shift to alternative means of energy?" When Obama dodged that question, Harwood asked again, "So could these high prices help us?"

"I think that I would have preferred a gradual adjustment," Obama said. "The fact that this is such a shock to American pocketbooks is not a good thing." In other words, raise prices slowly, not suddenly, but, clearly, raise them. [116]

That was also the view of Stephen Chu, Obama's Energy Secretary. Before joining the Obama administration, he called for a gradual increase in gas taxes over 15 years to goad consumers into buying fuel-efficient cars. He even said the cost of gas should rise to levels in Europe.[117] Somehow that didn't disqualify Chu for service in Obama's cabinet.

40

The "Not Enough Oil" LIE

"But here's the thing about oil. We have about 2, maybe 3, percent of the world's proven oil reserves. We use 25 percent of the world's oil. So think about it. Even if we doubled the amount of oil that we produce, we'd still be short by a factor of five."[118] —BHO

The truth is that the U.S. has enormous reserves available to us. "Proven" oil reserves is a technical term designating oil "that has been discovered (and) is economically and commercially viable," according to the American Petroleum Institute.[119] The actual oil domestically recoverable is enormous. The Institute for Energy Research reports that we have 1.4 trillion barrels that could be extracted using existing technology.[120] That includes offshore reserves, Alaska, and shale deposits in the western United Sates.

We are an energy rich nation. The problem America faces is not a lack of oil, but barriers to domestic production erected by environmental lobbyists (aka "influence peddlers") with the active cooperation of the President and his administration. The President wants us to embrace a green future and has put the brakes on offshore drilling where just 3 percent of our underwater areas are leased for energy production.[121] He has also closed public lands to oil shale development despite the enormous promise this has to meet our energy needs and reduce oil imports.

America now produces some 6 million barrels of oil a day. Mr. Obama could increase that by almost 2 million, a 25 percent increase, simply by opening federal lands to shale oil and tar sands production, which would produce 1 million barrels daily (and more in the future), and by authorizing the Keystone Oil pipeline project, which would bring 700,000 barrels of oil daily into America from Canada.[122] Our problem is not a lack of oil—it's our President and his "green" at all costs ideology.

41

The "Yes, We're Drilling" DECEPTION

"We are drilling at a record pace.... If you start hearing this 'drill, baby, drill' ... we're doing that. Tell me something new."[123] —BHO

Oil production is growing in America, but not because of Obama. He thinks oil is the energy source of the past and wants America to explore alternative sources. One way to force us to do so is to drive up prices, something his energy policy is helping to achieve. Remember, Obama chose an Energy secretary, Steven Chu, who said, "Somehow we have to figure out how to boost the price of gasoline to the levels in Europe."

The "record pace" of drilling of which Obama speaks is not taking place on federally controlled areas where Obama administration policy has sharply reduced oil production, but on private and state lands. North Dakota oil production on state and private land has surged from 2 million barrels ten years ago to a predicted 16 million barrels this year. The state just passed OPEC member Ecuador in its monthly oil production. The Bison state oil bonanza helps to make up for the reduced oil production off federal lands where, according to energy analyst Mario Loyola, production is down almost one million barrels a day.[124] Federal restrictions on Gulf of Mexico drilling will drop oil production by 700,000 barrels a day by the end of 2012, according to the Department of Energy. And data from the Institute for Energy Research reveals that on federal lands where Obama's policies hold sway there was a precipitous drop of about 40 percent in oil leases, permits, and wells in 2009-2010, compared to 2007-2008.[125] When it comes to domestic oil production, "We're doing that," but he's not.

42

"EPA Gives Us a Brighter Future" DECEPTION

"Our environment is safer because of you. Our country is stronger because of you. Our future is brighter because of you."[126] —**BHO**

Obama praised EPA workers on January 12, 2012, telling them America is safer, stronger, and enjoys a brighter future as a consequence of their work. Tell that to Idaho couple Michael and Chantell Sackett, forced to spend five years fighting an EPA order that declared their vacant .63 acre lot a "wetland" and off limits to construction. The Sacketts wanted to build a three-bedroom home on the lot, which has no standing water and sits in a residential area. They obtained local permits and work was already underway when the EPA showed up and issued a "compliance order" telling them to restore the land to its original condition. The environmental agency threatened the Sacketts with ruinous fines of up to $37,500 a day if they didn't comply.[127]

The Sacketts were denied a hearing to challenge the order until they first spent thousands of dollars to restore the property, and obtained a federal permit to build their home. It took five years, but a unanimous U.S. Supreme Court ruled on March 21, 2012, that landowners like the Sacketts have the right to direct, meaningful judicial review when their property is effectively seized by the EPA and declared a "wetland."

43

The "Green Jobs" LIE

"We'll invest $15 billion a year over the next decade in renewable energy, creating five million new green jobs...."[128] —BHO

The Obama administration has spent more than $90 billion in an attempt to generate the millions of "green jobs" candidate Obama promised in 2008. It hasn't worked. "Three years and nearly a hundred billion dollars later, taxpayers have received little return from President Obama's investments in 'green jobs,'" according to a scathing House Oversight and Government Reform Committee report on the President's green jobs agenda.[129]

For example, a $500 million stimulus program grant to "train and prepare individuals for careers in 'green jobs'" yielded little, if any, economic benefit, according to a Labor Department Inspector General report released last fall. The IG report found that after spending $168 million the Employment and Training Administration had trained 53,000 of the 125,000 workers called for in the grant and produced dismal results. Just 8,035 workers had found jobs, and a mere 1,033 were still at work after six months.[130] The IG report recommended that the remaining unspent funds be returned to the federal treasury "as soon as practicable and to the extent permitted by law."

Another $535 million in loan guarantees given to solar energy firm Solyndra may be lost since it declared bankruptcy and laid off 1,100 workers in September 2011. The *New York Times* called the President's promise of five million green jobs a "pipe dream" and said "Federal and state efforts to stimulate creation of green jobs have largely failed...."[131]

44

The "Climate Change and Carbon Tax" DECEPTION

"I am absolutely certain that generations from now, we will be able to look back and tell our children that this was the moment when ... the rise of the oceans began to slow and our planet began to heal."[132]
—BHO

Obama believes climate change is "one of the greatest moral challenges of our generation." Despite growing skepticism about man-caused global warming, Obama almost succeeded in 2009 in codifying a carbon regime into law that would have cost taxpayers billions of dollars and placed an enormous burden on the already strained U.S. economy. With the BP oil catastrophe, Obama bolstered his push to forward his socialist agenda, sabotage the U.S. economy, and burden Americans with a carbon tax. A study by the National Association of Manufacturers projected that a carbon tax would potentially decrease U.S. GDP by up to $269 billion and cost 850,000 jobs by 2014.

Many experts have questioned the scientific basis for imposing such a tax. Even if we did face a warming cataclysm, all the "carbon taxes" in the world would not be our salvation, these experts say. Additionally, the credibility of global warming "experts" has come into question due to the "Climategate" scandal, which revealed deceit and falsification by leading scientific advocates of the man-caused global warming theory. And even as the public cooled in their support of climate change legislation Obama's

Environmental Protection Agency (EPA) has moved to regulate carbon as a pollutant, imposing carbon taxes by the back door at a huge cost to jobs and businesses. Obama will stop at nothing to further his socialist agenda, which is why he rejects calls for increased domestic oil and nuclear production while promoting an ideological energy crisis that forces costly "green solutions" on society.

45

The "Save You ... $8,000 A Year" DECEPTION

"Now, because of these new standards for cars and trucks...over time, that saves you, a typical family, about $8,000 a year.... $8,000, that's no joke!" [133] —BHO

It would be easy to assume that Obama simply made a forgivable error when he boasted that new 55 mpg fuel efficiency standards will save families $8,000 annually. The projected fuel savings are actually $8,200 over the life of the vehicle, so it's possible that he or his speech writers just made a simple mistake. But in light of the fibs, falsehoods, and fabrications chronicled in this booklet, we have our doubts. And he was using a teleprompter.

Here's the math. The average driver spends $1,745 annually at today's price of gas. Doubling fuel efficiency standards, as the President said, would save $870 a year, not $8,000. Of course, if fuel prices continue to rise, it's possible that buyers will save $8,000 annually, as Obama promised. But we'd have to see prices of $37/gallon in order for that kind of savings to be realized.[134] Not too likely, even with the limits Obama has placed on oil production on federally controlled lands.

Whatever the actual savings in fuel over the life of a vehicle from the new standards, the cost to auto manufacturers of making more fuel efficient cars will add $3,100 to the purchase price of a new vehicle by 2025, according to an EPA estimate.[135] That added cost means less net financial benefit to drivers. It also will put new cars out or reach for some. A National Automobile Dealers Association estimate predicts 6.8 million drivers will be unable to get new car loans as a result.

46

The "I'm For Clean Coal" DECEPTION

"I know that West Virginia struggles with unemployment. That's part of the reason why I've said that we need a comprehensive energy policy that sets us up for a long-term future. For example, nobody has been a bigger promoter of clean coal technology than I am."[136] —BHO

During his campaign, candidate Obama was no friend to the coal industry, telling one interviewer that "if somebody wants to build a coal plant, they can — it's just that it will bankrupt them, because they are going to be charged a huge sum for all that greenhouse gas that's being emitted."[137] In an unguarded moment on the campaign trail, running mate Joe Biden piled on, announcing, "We're not supporting clean coal," and "No coal plants here in America." Still, Obama did try to make amends with coal states like West Virginia by promising in his "Blueprint for Change" to "enter into public private partnerships to develop" clean coal. And on the eve of his inauguration the incoming Obama administration signaled that coal would continue to be a "vital resource" for the nation.

But that talk didn't necessarily translate to action. The EPA, for example, issued in December 2011 a costly coal plant emission clean up mandate expected to cost the coal industry some $12 billion and hundreds of jobs. West Virginia Sen. Jay Rockefeller complained openly about the gap between Obama's sometime pro-coal rhetoric and actions taken by his administration at a Senate hearing on February 4, 2010. A somewhat put-out Rockefeller questioned both the president's candor and his credibility: "He says it in his speeches, but he doesn't say it in (his budget proposal). He doesn't say it in the actions of (EPA Administrator) Lisa Jackson. And he doesn't say it in the minds of my own people. And he's beginning to not be believable to me."[138] *Et tu*, Senator?

47

The "I Support Marriage" LIE

"I believe that marriage is the union between man and woman."[139] —BHO

That's what candidate Obama told evangelicals gathered at a candidate's forum at pastor Rick

Warren's Saddleback church in August 2008. But two months earlier, Obama sent a letter to the LGBT (Lesbian, Gay, Bisexual, Transsexual) Democratic Club announcing that he was "proud to join with and support the LGBT community in an effort to set our nation on a course that recognizes LGBT Americans with full equality under the law. That is why I support extending fully equal rights and benefits to same sex couples under both state and federal law. That is why I support repealing the Defense of Marriage Act...."[140]

Obama has sought the "complete repeal" of DOMA since his time in the U.S. Senate. As president, he further undermined DOMA by declaring it unconstitutional and ordering the U.S. Justice Department to drop its legal defense in two federal lawsuits—a dramatic move to abandon marriage and abdicate his sworn duty to "faithfully execute the office of President of the United States" Mr. Obama now says that "feelings are constantly evolving" on homosexual marriage—a signal he will soon embrace homosexual "marriage." It was said of Bill Clinton that he was the first "black" president. Mr. Obama's action well qualify him to be America's first "gay" president.

48

The "I'd Ban Infanticide" DECEPTION

"I would have been completely ... in support of the federal bill that everybody supported...that you should provide assistance to any infant that was born — even if it was as a consequence of an

induced abortion." [141] —BHO

Barack Obama voted "No" three times while in the Illinois Senate against a measure to protect children born alive after a failed abortion. The bill required doctors to provide these babies with medical care instead of leaving them to die. Obama opposed this ban on infanticide and helped kill the Illinois Born-Alive Infant Protection Act (Senate Bill 1082) in committee. Why? Obama said providing living babies outside the womb with "the kinds of protections that would be provided to a child" would cross a line "in terms of unconstitutionality" because it would treat the unborn as a person.

Candidate Obama lied about his record and claimed he would have supported the widely supported federal Born-Alive Infant Protection Act. He accused the National Right to Life Committee of lying when it charged that the state measure he opposed was identical to the federal infant protection measure. But legislative documents released by NRLC demonstrate that "Obama had, in fact, presided over the meeting at which the bill was transformed into a clone of the federal bill, and then voted down." National Right to Life Committee lobbyist Douglas Johnson said Obama "really did object to a bill merely because it defended the proposition, 'A live child born as a result of an abortion shall be fully recognized as a human person and accorded immediate protection under the law.'"[142] And then he lied to cover up his willingness to support abortion up to and including infanticide.

Section Five
ObamaCare Lies

It was his signature piece of legislature and the most audacious political initiative in U.S. history. He had the votes in the Democrat-controlled Congress to pass it, thanks to the Louisiana Purchase, the Corn Husker Kickback, and other backroom deals. But he never won over the U.S. public. A CNN poll taken the weekend ObamaCare passed found 59 percent of Americans opposed this massive government takeover. And that despite a long list of lies marshaled by Mr. Obama as he pressed his case. He tried to doctor the truth, but the public had no patience. Here are lies, damned lies, and ObamaCare lies.

49

The "47 Million Without Health Insurance" LIE

"This is not just about the 47 million Americans who don't have any health insurance at all."[143] —BHO

President Obama repeatedly claimed there are some 47 million uninsured Americans during the health care "reform" debate. It's a striking number useful to underscore our alleged health care crisis and to scare people witless. It's also false. While the Census Bureau's 2009 Current Population Survey (CPS) did report 46.3 million uninsured for 2008, the number of *Americans* who *cannot* obtain insurance is much smaller.

Here's a breakdown of the uninsured as provided by health care expert Sally Pipes. First, some 9.7 million people included among the uninsured earn upwards of $75,000 a year, suggesting they could pay for health insurance if they wished to. Second, 14 million qualify for various government health care programs but elect not to enroll. Third, 6 million are eligible for employer-provided insurance but don't take it. Fourth, 5 million of the uninsured are recent legal immigrants who have not yet bought health insurance. And fifth, 5.2 million are illegal immigrants. "Assuming some overlap with these numbers," Pipes writes, "there are, at most, 10 million U.S. citizens who lack affordable health care options, a much less scary figure."[144]

The actual number may be even less for two reasons. First, the Census Bureau itself acknowledges that "health insurance coverage is likely to be underreported in the CPS."[145] Second, many lack health insurance only temporarily as they seek work, change jobs, or enter the job market as young people. All in all, not quite the crisis he claimed.

50

The "Health Insurance Horror Story" LIE

"I will never forget my own mother, as she fought cancer in her final months, having to worry about whether her insurance would refuse to pay for her treatment."[146] — BHO

First as a candidate and then as President, Obama moved audiences with the emotional story of his mother's deathbed fight with her health insurance provider. As Obama told it, the insurer refused to pay for treatments because her cancer was a pre-existing condition. Not true, according to Janny Scott, author of a 2011 biography of Obama's mother, Ann Dunham. Scott writes that Dunham had health insurance which "covered most of the costs of her medical treatment.... The hospital billed her insurance company directly, leaving Ann to pay only the deductible and any uncovered expenses, which, she said, came to several hundred dollars a month."[147]

Dunham did battle her disability insurance provider, Cigna, over whether her cancer was a pre-existing condition that made her ineligible for disability payments. But that's not what Obama told the nation as he used his compelling health insurance horror story to help pass ObamaCare. As Scott reports: "Though he often suggested that she was denied health coverage because of a pre-existing condition, it appears from her correspondence that she was only denied disability coverage."[148]

Scott's 2011 book came too late to impeach the President's claim during the ObamaCare debate in Congress but, oddly, he's still using it. Narrator Tom Hanks intones a carefully phrased version of the faux account in the richly produced Obama campaign biopic, "The Road We've Traveled." *Washington Post* "Fact Checker" Glenn Kessler took a look and concluded that it gave a "misleading impression of what really happened." His verdict? Three Pinocchios.[149]

51

The "ObamaCare Is Not A Tax" LIE

"No. That's not true George.... For us to say that you've got to take a responsibility to get health insurance is absolutely not a tax increase.... I absolutely reject that notion."[150] —BHO

During the ObamaCare debate President Obama and his team repeatedly insisted that the mandates in the ObamaCare law were not, in fact, tax increases. On September 20, 2009, during an interview with ABC News's George Stephanopoulos, Obama flatly rejected the charge that ObamaCare amounted to a tax increase: "That's not true, George... For us to say that you've got to take a responsibility to get health insurance is absolutely not a tax increase." After repeated questioning on the issue, Stephanopoulos asked in conclusion, "You reject that it's a tax increase?" Obama replied, "I absolutely reject that notion."[151] To admit the obvious would have forced the President into the very uncomfortable acknowledgement that ObamaCare violates his promise to not raise taxes on those making less than $250,000. As Yale Law School professor Jack M. Balkin, an ObamaCare supporter, told an audience, the President "has not been honest with the American people about the nature of this bill. **This bill is a tax.**"[152]

After ObamaCare's passage and as the legal challenges to the new law mounted, Obama and his legal team changed course and instead built their legal defense on the government's "power to lay and collect taxes."[153] This is classic Obama politics. Knowing the tax argument would have caused the ObamaCare bill to be listed as the largest tax increase in American history — making passage very difficult — Obama rejected the tax label only to embrace it as his legal defense. This is Obama at his lying, double-speaking best.

52

The "Not Socialized Medicine" LIE

"When you hear people saying, 'socialized medicine,' understand that I do not know anybody in Washington who is proposing that–certainly not me."[154] —BHO

Not just the president, but many in the media, went to great lengths during the ObamaCare debate to deny that Mr. Obama's health care plan meant socialized medicine. One writer even called that claim reminiscent of "worries about fluoride in the water."[155]

So what is socialized medicine? It's when "government controls medical resources and socializes the costs."[156] By that definition ObamaCare fully qualifies as socialized medicine. It places 18 percent of the U.S. economy under the tight supervision of federal bureaucrats and makes the purchase of health insurance compulsory for everyone. It also dictates the benefits Americans must buy in their health policies and tells private health insurers what policies to sell, to whom, and for how much. Anyone who doubts that should ask insurers who are now required to provide free contraceptives, sterilizations, and abortion-causing drugs to employees of firms with which they contract – all without regard to the moral objections of the insurer or the insured.

Health policy expert Peter Ferrara calls ObamaCare "nothing short of a government takeover of health care"—something known in other countries as "socialized medicine." One of those nations is Cuba, which has had government-run health care—and a struggling economy—for decades. The island nation's dictator, Fidel Castro, praised ObamaCare's passage, calling it a "success" for President Obama. Castro said he found it "really incredible that 234 years after the Declaration of Independence" America has done "something that Cuba was able to do half a century ago."[157]

53

The "ObamaCare Means Savings For Families" LIE

"I also have a health care plan that would save the average family $2,500 on their premiums."[158] —BHO

Obama repeatedly promised in 2008 that his health insurance revamp would put money back in families' pockets, saving them $2,500 a year. Somehow expanding the list of treatments health plans must cover and dropping the out-of-pocket costs for care would prompt insurance companies to lower their rates.

It's not working out as Obama promised. Premiums are already going up. The cost on average of an employer-provided family health plan grew five percent in both 2008 and 2009, and just three percent in 2010. But in 2011, as ObamaCare mandates started to take effect, costs exploded, rising 9 percent to $15,000 per family. Things will only get worse in 2014 when the law takes full effect. Jonathan Gruber, an MIT economist who helped Obama create his plan (and earlier helped craft Romney care in Massachusetts) predicts, for example, that the cost to some Wisconsin consumers in the individual market will rise 31 percent. Some consumers in the Ohio individual market could face rate hikes of 55 to 85 percent.[159]

Insurance premiums are rising under ObamaCare because of its expensive coverage mandates, its $500 billion in new taxes, and the increased regulatory burden imposed by the new law. The Congressional Budget Office estimates that a workplace insurance policy for a family of four will cost $20,000 by 2016. Health care consumers in the individual market, according to CBO, will face prices at least $2,100 more than if ObamaCare had not passed.[160]

54

The "No Death Panels" LIE

Death panels? "It is a lie, plain and simple."[161]
—BHO

President Obama blasted critics of ObamaCare who claim, he said, that "we plan to set up panels of bureaucrats with the power to kill off senior citizens." Such claims are "bogus" and a "lie, plain and simple."[162]

But Obama revealed the future of health care when he told a woman whose healthy 105 year-old mother had a pacemaker implanted at age 99 that, "we actually have some — some choices to make about how we want to deal with our own end-of-life care." When it comes to tough end-of-life health care choice, Obama said, "at least we can let doctors know and your mom know that, you know what? Maybe this isn't going to help. Maybe you're better off not having the surgery, but taking the painkiller."[163] Translation: We, the government will tell your doctor and your mom: "Sorry, no surgery, take the pill."

No wonder former Alaska governor Sarah Palin charged that ObamaCare would lead to health care rationing decisions made by bureaucrats, or "Obama's 'death panel.'"

Now we learn that ObamaCare really does have a panel of bureaucrats empowered to make life-or-death decisions about health care spending. The Independent Payment Advisory Board (IPAB) is a 15-member panel of medical experts created by the health law to limit Medicare spending and make decisions to withhold or provide treatments. IPAB's rulings are insulated from public and political pressure, and are not subject to judicial review. It takes House action, a 60-vote Senate super-majority, and the President's signature to overturn IPAB "recommendations." Liberal House member Pete Stark warns that IPAB will "endanger the health of America's seniors and people with disabilities." And Tennessee Congressman Phil Roe, who has practiced medicine for 30 years, calls it the "real death panel."

IPAB cost-cutting, set to take effect in 2015, could

in fact lead to death for those in need of life-saving care. Medicare spending cuts in Arizona have already led to the death of two people awaiting transplants. And budget conscious bureaucrats at Oregon state-run health insurance plan refused in 2008 to cover the cost of treatment for two cancer patients. They did, however, offer to pay for much-less expensive doctor-assisted suicides.[164]

55

"No Single-Payer System" LIE

"What are not legitimate concerns are those being put forward claiming a public option is somehow a Trojan horse for a single-payer system...."[165] —BHO

In a June 2009 speech to the American Medical Association (AMA), President Obama fiercely denied that his health proposal's "public option" (a government-run insurance plan that competes against private health insurers) would lead to universal health care in America. Mr. Obama's Democrat colleagues knew better. Rep. Barney Frank, then chairman of the House Financial Services Committee, said a month later, "I think the best way we're going to get single payer, the only way, is to have a public option and demonstrate the strength of its power." Rep. Jan Schakowsky was equally frank. She told a cheering crowd that "A public option will put the private insurance industry out of business and lead to single-payer."[166] Likewise, Sen. Russ Feingold told an interviewer during the debate that while single-payer wasn't in the cards then, "I believe that the goal here is to create whatever legislation we have in a way that could be developed into something like a single-payer system."[167]

While public resistance killed the public option, ObamaCare requires the Office of Personnel Management to create at least two government health care plans that will compete against private insurance. That's the public option by stealth and a fast track to a single payer system, something Obama promised in 2007, stating that "as President I will sign a universal health care plan into law by the end of my first term in office."[168]

56

The "ObamaCare Deficit-Neutral" LIE

"I have pledged that health insurance reform will not add one dime to our deficit over the next decade, and I mean it."[169]—BHO

ObamaCare will provide coverage to 32 million or more presently uninsured people, but the President wants us to believe his government healthcare takeover will have no negative bottom-line impact on the federal budget. He says he'll make up for the increased cost by improved efficiencies but when does government do anything efficiently?

Estimates vary about the true ten-year cost of ObamaCare, running from $383 billion (Centers for Medicare and Medicaid Services) to $3 trillion (Cato Institute). The Congressional Budget Office doubled its original estimate in March 2012. The CBO now says that ObamaCare will cost the nation $1.76 trillion between 2012 and 2022. No one knows for certain, but no one with any political candor still thinks it will be deficit neutral. One thing for sure. The cost of ObamaCare, unless repealed, will vastly outstrip official estimates. We were told in 1965, for example, that Medicare would cost taxpayers just $12 billion by 1990. Actual cost that year was $109.7 billion—815 percent above projection.

One of the most worrisome and most likely cost impacts from ObamaCare will come as employers dump workers into taxpayer subsidized healthcare exchanges. And why not? The employer cost per worker for family coverage is $15,000 (and climbing) while the federal penalty to employers for not providing healthcare insurance is just $2,000. Look for at least half of all companies to send their workers to the government-run exchanges which will mean an annual cost to taxpayers of $400 billion by 2021.[170] As the authors of *Why ObamaCare Is Wrong for America* warn, health care "reform" is "a budget buster of historic proportions," one that "will add trillions of dollars to government spending in the coming years."

57

The "No Medicare Cuts" LIE

"So I just want to assure, we're not talking about cutting Medicare benefits."[171] —BHO

Au contraire. Despite the president's glib assurance at a New Hampshire town hall meeting in 2009, we are, in fact, talking about huge cuts to Medicare under the health care takeover law. It slashes Medicare spending by some $800 billion in its first 10 years of actual implementation (2014-2023). That means less money for doctors and for treatments that seniors on Medicare need. The chief actuary of the Centers for Medicare and Medicaid Services warned that 15 percent of Medicare providers may become unprofitable because of the funding cuts and stop seeing Medicare patients as a result. As health policy expert Peter Ferrara puts it, "If the government is not going to pay, then seniors are not going to get the health services, treatment and care they expect."[172]

Congress has never made good on the politically hazardous step of cutting Medicare—until now. What's different is that ObamaCare creates a 15-member "Independent Payment Advisory Board" that is fully immunized from political pressure and charged under the law with insuring that Medicare spending targets in ObamaCare take effect. Bottom line, Medicare will be cut and seniors will find themselves unable to see doctors or obtain treatments as a result.

58

The "Keep Your Insurance" LIE

"Here's a guarantee that I have made. If you have insurance that you like, then you will be able to keep that insurance."[173] —BHO

This "guarantee" is listed in the "Reality Check" section of the White House website. Maybe the time has come to quietly retire it because it is about to get mugged by reality. The truth is that up to half of all working Americans, some 78 million people, may find themselves without employer-sponsored health insurance once ObamaCare takes effect in 2014. It won't matter how much they like their old plan once employers conclude that the carrots and sticks built into ObamaCare make dropping health plans for workers a good business decision.

A 2011 McKinsey & Company survey[174] of 1,300 employers found that 30 percent of business owners say they will definitely or probably cancel their worker insurance plans. For employers well-informed about ObamaCare, the proportion who will stop providing worker health insurance jumps to 50 percent. McKinsey analyst Alissa Meade believes "something in the range of 80 million to 100 million individuals are going to change coverage categories in the two years" after 2014.

Costly new ObamaCare coverage mandates along with new taxes on expensive plans, and the fact that workers will have the option of buying health insurance in taxpayer subsidized "healthcare exchanges," will combine to make dumping workers an economic and acceptable decision for employers. But not for taxpayers. The cost of ObamaCare will explode if 78 million people take advantage of subsidized health plans. An analysis done by former Congressional Budget Office Director Douglas Holtz-Eakin found that it will cost $1.4 trillion over ten years if "just" 35 million people take advantage of subsidized health coverage.[175] Double that if the McKinsey estimate holds true.

59

The "We're Not Paying For Abortions In ObamaCare " LIE

"Under our plan, no federal dollars will be used to fund abortions...." [176] —BHO

It took the promise of an executive order supposedly banning abortion funding in ObamaCare to win over holdout "pro-life" House Democrats, and secure passage in March 2010 of the Patient Protection and Affordable Care Act, aka ObamaCare. But a mere four months later the administration was caught giving the green light to abortion in one of the many insurance programs created under ObamaCare.

"Without blinking, the Obama administration had approved high-risk pool plans submitted by at least three states that would have funded virtually all abortions – until NRLC raised the alarms," said National Right to Life Committee Legislative Director Douglas Johnson. Exposed, the administration reversed course and rejected abortion coverage under the Pre-Existing Condition Insurance Plan (PCIP), also known as the "high-risk pool" program. But the Obama administration left the door open for future funding of abortion. As White House Office of Health Reform head Nancy-Ann DeParle said at the time, the decision "is not a precedent for other programs or policies given the unique, temporary nature of the program...."[177]

And in March 2012, the Department of Health and Human Services issued a new rule revealing that Americans who qualify for a federal health care insurance subsidy will be able to buy health plans that provide abortions in the new health care exchanges set up under ObamaCare. The rule sets no limits on how late in pregnancy an abortion may be obtained or for what reasons. Enrollees in abortion-providing plans will be required to pay an "abortion surcharge" of at least $1 a month. NRLC calls that a "bookkeeping device that is intended to obscure the reality that the federal government will be purchasing abortion-on-demand insurance."

Johnson and colleague Susan Muskett write that "the new rule is only the latest evidence that pro-life objections to ObamaCare were well founded."[178]

60

The "Everyone's Doing It" LIE

"Nearly 99 percent of all women have relied on contraception at some point in their lives— 99 percent." [179] —BHO

Obama used his claim that nearly all American women use contraceptives to buttress his decision forcing insurers to provide free contraceptives, sterilizations, and abortion drugs through employer-provided health plans regardless of the employer's religious objections. Of course, if 99 percent of women already use contraceptives, one has to wonder why it's necessary to force insurers to provide them as freely as the condoms Planned Parenthood hands out gratis to teens and college students. That question aside, Obama's stat is simply false. First, 13.9 percent of women age 15-44 have never had heterosexual intercourse, according to a definitive government study of contraceptive use published by the Centers for Disease Control and Prevention.[180] That same study also found that 38.2 percent of women age 15-44 reported they were not currently using contraception. So not as universal as Obama made it sound.

His claim may have come, as CNSNews.com editor Terence Jeffrey points out, from "a careless or misleading restatement" of an Institute of Medicine report recommending that ObamaCare require health policies to provide free coverage for contraceptives.[181] The report says "More than 99 percent of U.S. women aged 15 to 44 years who have ever had sexual intercourse with a male have used at least one contraceptive method." But that's not "all women" as Obama claimed. Just those who have had heterosexual intercourse. Big difference.

61

The "ObamaCare Won't Violate Religious Rights" LIE

"Under our plan...federal conscience laws will remain in place."[182] —BHO

President Obama showed contempt for conscience rights and religious liberty on January 20, 2012 when his administration ordered that all group health insurance plans must cover, without a co-pay, contraceptives, sterilizations, and early abortion drugs.[183] The sweeping mandate included a sliver-thin exemption for which only a few churches or religious orders qualify. Catholic organizations protested loudly and the administration issued a "compromise" that requires health insurance firms to provide the mandatory services directly at no cost. "The so-called new policy is the discredited old policy, dressed up to look like something else," said New Jersey Representative Chris Smith. "It remains a serious violation of religious freedom."

The mandate must be implemented by August 1, 2012, and forces all organizations (including but not limited to Catholic and evangelical organizations) to choose between giving up their rights of conscience and paying fines of up to $2,000 per worker. Colorado Christian University, which is suing to overturn the mandate, will be forced to pay $500,000 for the privilege of staying true to its religious moral convictions unless a federal judge intervenes.

Health and Human Services Secretary Kathleen Sebelius calls the mandate a good and proper compromise, saying "we are working to strike the right balance between respecting religious beliefs and increasing women's access to critical preventive health services." But since when did religious liberty, America's fundamental freedom, become something to be balanced against a guaranteed supply of free contraceptives and abortion drugs such as *Ella*? And there's no "balance" here; religious liberty is being crushed. In fact, Mr. Obama actively opposed the "Blunt amendment," a Senate measure to give employers the right to opt out of the edict on religious grounds. For him, it's birth control and abortion *uber alles*.

Section Six
Foreign Policy Lies

It's sometimes said that a diplomat is a man sent abroad to lie for his country. That certainly was true of Mr. Obama when he went to Cairo in 2009 to deliver a speech recasting Islam as an exemplar of tolerance. But Obama didn't need to leave home to lie. He's done that from his own front porch. He told Americans (and Israelis) that he has "Israel's back," misrepresented a legal action to remove the Honduran president as a coup, and claimed falsely to have banned torture and closed Gitmo. More examples of how Obama has tortured the truth.

62

The "Guantanamo Will Close" LIE

"The detention facilities at Guantanamo for individuals covered by this order shall be closed as soon as practicable, and no later than one year from the date of this order."[184] —BHO

Candidate Obama promised repeatedly to close the military detention facility at Guantanamo Bay, and two days after being sworn in as President, he signed an executive order calling for Guantanamo's closure within a year. There was joy in Liberalville that this "unjust" facility would soon be shuttered. "After the wilderness years of the Bush presidency, this seemed like the Promised Land," wrote left-wing activist Bianca Jagger in 2011. "Except, of course, it wasn't."

More than three years after his executive order, Obama has not made good on his promise to close the prison for terrorists, an outcome for which freedom and peace-loving people can be thankful. Resistance in Congress and public reaction to moving Al Qaeda terrorists to a high-security detention facility in Illinois and to the prospect of trying 9/11 plotter Khalid Sheikh Mohammed in New York City helped stymie the President's plan to close Gitmo. He effectively conceded that Guantanamo will not be closed on March 7, 2011 when he issued another executive order to resume military trials at Guantanamo and establish a "periodic review" process for detainees not charge or convicted but deemed to be still at war with the U.S.

63

The "I Have Israel's Back" LIE

"No U.S. administration has done more in support of Israel's security than ours. None." [185] —BHO

Candidate Obama pledged his "unshakeable commitment to Israel's security" in 2008 and claimed in 2012 that when the chips are down, "I have Israel's back."[186] But U.S.-Israeli relations have been troubled throughout Obama's tenure. He sees the Palestinian conflict as the key to resolving Middle East tensions and has been largely pro-Palestinian in his approach to Israel. He implied a moral equivalence between Jewish persecution over centuries, including the

Holocaust, and the cause of the Palestinians who, he said, "have suffered in pursuit of a homeland."

President Obama showed his pro-Arab, anti-Israel bias almost immediately after taking office when his first trip to the Middle East did not include a stop in Israel but instead focused on his Egypt visit and Cairo speech. Obama has pressured Israel to stop settlements while making few demands on Palestinians. When Israeli authorities issued a permit to build in an area of Jerusalem that Israel has never considered contested territory, the U.S. State Department heavily criticized the Jewish state. And the Obama administration refused to veto a rushed U.N. resolution condemning Israel just 24 hours after Israeli commandos boarded vessels attempting to ferry Palestinian activists into Gaza in May 2010. Most egregiously, the President has publicly called for Israel to return to its pre-1967 borders, which would leave the nation just nine miles wide at its narrowest point and "indefensible," as Netanyahu told the President in a joint Oval Office press conference. As columnist Charles Krauthammer said, "This President has done more to delegitimize and undermine Israel's position in the world than any other President."[187]

64

The "Jerusalem" LIE

"Jerusalem will remain the capital of Israel, and it must remain undivided."[188] —BHO

Barack Obama issued this pledge to the American Israel Public Affairs Committee in 2008 as he stumped for the Jewish vote in his bid to be President. His promise sparked fury across the Middle East. Palestinian Authority President Mahmoud Abbas rejected Obama's statement, saying "holy Jerusalem was occupied in 1967 and we will not accept a Palestinian state without having Jerusalem as the capital of a Palestinian state." Obama got the message and backed away from his pledge within hours, telling CNN, "Well, obviously, it's going to be up to the parties to negotiate a range of these issues. And Jerusalem will be part of those negotiations." [189]

As President, Mr. Obama further contradicted his 2008 promise by calling for Israel to return to its 1967 borders, a dramatic redrawing of the map which would make Israel indefensible and divide Israel's capital city by placing East Jerusalem under Palestinian control. The Obama administration has even refused to put the words "Jerusalem, Israel" on the passports of U.S. citizens born in Jerusalem and has scrubbed references to "Jerusalem, Israel" from the White House website so as not to endorse Israel's claim to its capital.

When Barack beat a hasty retreat from his 2008 AIPAC pledge, Morton A. Klein, National President of the Zionist Organization of America observed, "One must question whether his initial remark was simply meant to mislead Jewish voters and Israel supporters by not stating his true beliefs on this issue."[190] You think?

65

The "Muslims Are Tolerant" LIE

"And throughout history, Islam has demonstrated through words and deeds the possibilities of religious tolerance and racial equality." —BHO

Sorry, Mr. President, there is no Muslim nation to which one can point as a shining example of tolerance and racial equality. Take Saudi Arabia, the birthplace of Islam. It, more than any other Muslim land, ought to showcase the acceptance and diversity of which Obama spoke so glowingly in his Cairo address to the Muslim world. In fact, the homeland of Mohammad offers zero tolerance for other religions. The Muslim state prohibits churches and gives apostates from Islam the death penalty, as required by the Koran. And don't say a word against Islam or Mohammad—that's blasphemy, also a capital crime.

Similar restrictions apply now across the Muslim world and have been in force since the seventh century when Mohammad began to spread Islam through military conquest. Non-Muslims who survived under the Muslim empire that stretched from Spain to India lived as subjugated members of society, or Dhimmis, as author Ba'at Yeor has powerfully chronicled. According to Jadunath Sarkar, a historian of Muslim rule in India: "The conversion of the entire population to Islam and the extinction of every form of dissent is the ideal of the Muslim State.... A non-Muslim therefore cannot be a citizen of the State; he is a member of a depressed class; his status is a modified form of slavery."[191] All this stems directly from the Koran which instructs believers to take up arms against infidels: "O Prophet! Strive hard against the unbelievers and the hypocrites, and be firm against them." (Qu'ran 9:73). Not much religious tolerance there.

66

The "I'm Not Really Apologizing For America" LIE

[Koran burning apology] *"calmed things down."* [192] —BHO

The families of two U.S. military officers killed after President Obama made this claim would likely disagree about the soothing effects of his "we-a culpa," delivered to Afghanistan president Hamid Karzai for the burning of several copies of the Koran. So would a group of senior Afghan Muslim clerics who dismissed the President's apology, which came three days after news of the Feb. 20, 2012, Koran burning became public, sparking riots and deaths inside Afghanistan.

The incident occurred after U.S. military officials discovered detainees at a prison located at Baghram air base writing messages on the pages of prison library Korans as a means of communicating with each other. The scribbled-in copies of the Koran were reportedly removed and burned because they were defaced and because of a lack of storage space.

But neither those factors, nor the President's apology, made any difference to the Muslim leaders. While saying nothing about the six U.S. military personnel murdered by Afghans upset about the burning, the clerics called the Koran incident "an unforgivable act ... it will certainly not going to be forgiven by apologies, the responsible parties should be prosecuted in an open trial and they should be punished."[193] So much for calming things down.

67

The "No Blame for the Past" LIE

"It is our intention to assure those who carried out their duties relying in good faith upon legal advice from the Department of Justice that they will not be subject to prosecution."[194] —BHO

That April 16, 2009, "promise" from President Obama assuring no prosecutions for intelligence officers who conducted harsh terrorist interrogations to protect America didn't last long. Four months after Obama said "nothing will be gained by spending our time and energy laying blame for the past," his Attorney General, Eric Holder, decided he would do just that. Holder appointed a prosecutor to look into allegations already reviewed and dismissed by career prosecutors in the Bush Justice Department.

Holder's re-investigation came despite pleas from seven former CIA directors asking the President to abandon the probe. The directors warned that re-opening already investigated charges would place "costly financial and other burdens" on intelligence community members and "seriously damage the willingness of many other intelligence officers to take risks to protect the country."[195] Then-CIA

Director Leon Panetta also objected to a renewed investigation in a "profanity-laced screaming match" at the White House.

Two years later, Holder announced that he had turned up nothing and all but two cases would be closed. The damage, however, from a "witch hunt" Obama promised would never take place is "incalculable" said Marc Thiessen, a former speechwriter for Secretary of Defense Don Rumsfeld: "Some of our most talented, capable counterterrorism officials have left government service — and countless others, who might have contemplated such service, have chosen other careers instead."[196] And who knows what price we will all pay for that in years ahead.

68

The "Coup in Honduras" LIE

"We believe that the coup was not legal and that President Zelaya remains the president of Honduras, the democratically elected president there."[197]
—BHO

When the Honduran Congress removed President Manuel Zelaya from power on June 28, 2009, and the army sent him out of the country, President Obama quickly labeled the action an illegal coup. He called it a "terrible precedent," and demanded his return to power. So did Fidel Castro and Hugo Chavez, Venezuela's dictator for life, who had been aiding Zelaya's effort to hold a constitutional referendum on whether he could serve beyond the

Constitution's one-term limit. Chavez even supplied printed ballots for the referendum to keep Zelaya in power and expand Chavez' regional influence.

But Zelaya's link to Chavez didn't seem to matter to the Obama administration, which heavily pressured tiny Honduras to restore Zelaya to power by suspending visa services for Hondurans, threatening to cut off $135 million in aid, and supporting the expulsion of Honduras from the Organization of American States. [198]

Honduras refused to buckle and for good reason. It wasn't a coup as Obama claimed. Article 239 of the Honduras Constitution limits the presidency to one four-year term and requires the removal of public officials who propose changing that rule. Honduras' Congress, which is vested with the power to remove the president, acted accorded to the law, as the Congressional Research Service at the Library of Congress confirmed in an August 2009 report.[199]

69

The "I Have Banned Torture" LIE

"The fear and anger that [9/11] provoked was understandable, but in some cases, it led us to act contrary to our ideals. We are taking concrete actions to change course. I have unequivocally prohibited the use of torture by the United States." [200] —BHO

Torture was already illegal in the U.S. before Obama signed an executive order on January 22, 2009, changing the rules by which U.S. interrogation officers may go about their business. The order revokes the Bush-era legal understanding that allowed enhanced interrogation techniques. These coercive methods were employed in just 100 or so cases according to former CIA director Michael Hayden. Waterboarding, which Mr. Obama defines as torture, was only used against three Al Qaeda leaders, all of whom broke and gave information used to defeat terror plots.

Mr. Obama's pious claim to have prohibited the use of torture made in his Cairo speech to the Muslim world ratified their assumptions about U.S. misdeeds since 9/11. In suggesting that "fear and anger" caused us to "act contrary to our ideals" after 9/11, Obama was, once more, taking a swipe at President George W. Bush and the course of U.S. security policy since nearly 3,000 Americans were killed on 9/11.

It was worse than a swipe. It was slander because it was untrue. We didn't violate our principles to wage war against terrorists. "That simply wasn't the case," Vice President Dick Cheney told CNN. "We were never torturing anyone in the first place."[201] The interrogation techniques employed did, however, help keep Americans safe after 9/11. Whether we will remain safe without this tool to fight terror remains to be seen.

Endnotes

1. http://www.washingtontimes.com/weblogs/joe-curl/2009/Mar/08/obama-makes-oval-office-call-reporters/

2. http://newsbusters.org/blogs/michael-m-bates/2009/03/08/new-york-times-some-conservatives-have-implied-obamas-socialist

3. http://www.forbes.com/2010/02/24/obama-remarks-economy-business-beltway-government_2.html

4. http://www.whitehouse.gov/the-press-office/2011/12/06/remarks-president-economy-osawatomie-kansas

5. http://heartland.org/policy-documents/bast-american-prosperity-kennedy-reagan

6. http://www.sojo.net/blogs/2012/02/21/transcript-barack-obama-and-god-factor-interview

7. http://www.thaindian.com/newsportal/politics/face-to-face-with-george-hussein-obama-barack-obamas-brother_10099079.html

8. http://www.bloomberg.com/apps/news?pid=newsarchive&sid=a.dMoapeTcME&refer=us

9. http://documents.nytimes.com/president-obamas-2008-income-tax-returns

10. http://blogs.suntimes.com/sweet/2011/04/obama_2011_tax_returns.html

11. http://www.youtube.com/watch?v=uAQdQtB4WvY&feature=related, at :24 seconds.

12. http://www.youtube.com/watch?v=ni4X9Be-wwA

13. http://www.thedailybeast.com/newsweek/2009/04/06/one-nation-under-god.html

14. http://www.gallup.com/poll/151760/Christianity-Remains-Dominant-Religion-United-States.aspx

15. http://abcnews.go.com/Blotter/DemocraticDebate/story?id=4443788&page=1

16. http://www.mcclatchydc.com/2008/03/20/31079/obamas-church-pushes-controversial.html#storylink=cpy

17. Stanley Kurtz, Radical-in-Chief (New York: Simon & Schuster, 2010), 301.

18. http://www.nytimes.com/2008/04/29/us/politics/29text-obama.html?pagewanted=print

19. http://www.thedailybeast.com/newsweek/2008/

05/03/something-wasn-t-wright.html

20. Stanley Kurtz, Radical-in-Chief (New York: Simon & Schuster, 2010), 303.

21. http://thecaucus.blogs.nytimes.com/2008/05/29/obama-apologizes-for-another-pastor-critical-of-clinton/

22. http://blogs.suntimes.com/sweet/2008/05/pfleger_a_headache_for_obama_a.html

23. Kurtz, Stanley. Radical-in-Chief (Simon & Schuster, Inc., 2010), 253.

24. Ibid., 254.

25. http://sojo.net/blogs/2012/02/21/transcript-barack-obama-and-god-factor-interview

26. Ibid., 11.

27. http://www.politifact.com/truth-o-meter/statements/2009/sep/17/karl-rove/rove-claims-obama-used-to-be-lawyer-for-acorn/

28. http://obamalies.net/obama-flip-flops-on-acorn.html

29. http://www.foxnews.com/story/0,2933,587286,00.html; http://www.youtube.com/watch?v=q_nNG6wterg&feature=player_embedded

30. http://radio.woai.com/cc-common/news/sections/newsarticle.html?feed=119078&article=3301545#ixzz1p7GAUqq6

31. http://www.youtube.com/watch?v=EGjR81pFJI4

32. http://www.youtube.com/watch?v=_cv333saZoU

33. http://www.americanthinker.com/blog/2010/04/the_constitution_as_a_living_d.html

34. http://www.whitehouse.gov/the_press_office/TransparencyandOpenGovernment

35. http://www.politico.com/news/stories/0312/73606.html

36. http://www.freedominfo.org/2011/01/u-s-supreme-court-hears-corporate-privacy-case/

37. http://www.youtube.com/watch?v=o5t8GdxFYBU

38. http://www.cato.org/publications/techknowledge/promise-keeps-breaking

39. http://www.politifact.com/truth-o-meter/promises/obameter/promise/240/tougher-rules-against-revolving-door-for-lobbyists/

40. http://www.politifact.com/truth-o-meter/promises/obameter/promise/240/tougher-rules-against-revolving-door-for-lobbyists/

41. http://www.politifact.com/truth-o-meter/promises/promise/517/health-care-reform-public-sessions-C-SPAN/

42. http://www.politico.com/blogs/michaelcalderone/
    0110/CSPANs_Lamb_to_Congress_Open_health_c
    are_debate.html

43. http://www.mcclatchydc.com/2009/07/09/71584/
    obama-campaign-vow-of-public-debate.html

44. http://www.mcclatchydc.com/2009/07/09/71584/
    obama-campaign-vow-of-public-debate.html

45. http://www.politifact.com/truth-o-meter/promises/
    promise/512/go-line-line-over-
    earmarks-make-sure-money-being-s/

46. http://obama.3cdn.net/0080cc578614b42284_
    2a0mvyxpz.pdf

47. http://www.politifact.com/truth-o-meter/promises/
    obameter/promise/431/reduce-earmarks-to-1994-
    levels/

48. Read more here: http://www.mcclatchydc.com/
    2009/02/22/62614/earmark-reform-2009-spending-
    bill.html#storylink=cpy

49. http://www.guardian.co.uk/commentisfree/2008/
    nov/05/uselections2008-barackobama

50. http://reason.com/blog/2010/05/03/obama-fights-
    corporate-takeove

51. http://www.nationalreview.com/corner/290383/
    obama-campaign-embraces-threat-our-democracy-
    daniel-foster

52. http://cnsnews.com/news/article/obama-republi-
    cans-want-dirtier-air-dirtier-water-0

53. http://michellemalkin.com/2011/10/17/obama-
    republican-plan/

54. http://www.newyorker.com/reporting/2012/01/30
    /120130fa_fact_lizza#ixzz1pMxKltGo

55. http://www.newyorker.com/reporting/2012/01/30
    /120130fa_fact_lizza#ixzz1pN1ZYUna

56. Obama's "The Change We Need In Washington,"
    http://www.govexec.com/pdfs/092208ts1.pdf

57. David Limbaugh, Crime Against Liberty: An
    Indictment of President Barack Obama
    (Washington, D.C.: Regnery, 2010), 272.

58. http://news.investors.com/article/601526/201202
    171525/obama-economic-stimulus-turns-three.htm

59. http://www.bls.gov/news.release/empsit.t15.htm

60 http://www.sentierresearch.com/reports/Sentier_
    Research_Household_Income_Trends_Report_Janu
    ary_2012_12_03_01.pdf

61. http://www.nytimes.com/2009/04/29/us/politics/
    29text-obama.html?pagewanted=all

62. http://abcnews.go.com/blogs/politics/2009/05/
    the-stimulus-sa/

63. http://blog.heritage.org/2012/02/27/cbos-stimulus-review-as-good-as-a-horoscope/

64. http://www.realclearpolitics.com/2010/01/25/federal_spending_for_dummies_228342.html

65. http://www.cbo.gov/publication/42911

66. http://www.usatoday.com/news/washington/story/2012-01-31/obama-budget-deficit-report/52907098/1

67. http://www.foxnews.com/politics/2011/10/17/obama-first-1000-days/

68. http://www.presidency.ucsb.edu/ws/index.php?pid=85080&st=&st1=#axzz1pDlr3l5N

69. http://www.deseretnews.com/article/705357688/AP-Impact-Road-projects-dont-help-unemployment.html?pg=1

70. http://www.nytimes.com/2010/10/17/magazine/17obama-t.html?_r=3&ref=magazine&pagewanted=all"

71. http://hotair.com/archives/2010/10/16/brooks-hey-obama-told-me-shovel-ready-jobs-didnt-exist-last-year/

72. Ron Suskind, Confidence Men: Wall Street, Washington, and the Education of a President (New York: Harper, 2011).

73. http://www.usatoday.com/money/autos/2010-11-18-gm-obama_N.htm

74. http://www.newsmax.com/Economy/GM-Record-Profit-Obama/2011/12/23/id/421999

75. http://www.detroitnews.com/article/20120130/AUTO01/201300393

76. http://money.cnn.com/2012/02/28/news/economy/obama_auto_bailout/index.htm

77. http://www.forbes.com/sites/paulroderickgregory/2012/02/06/american-airlines-shows-the-corruption-of-obamas-gm-bailout/

78. http://abcnews.go.com/Politics/video?id=6866999

79. http://abcnews.go.com/Politics/video?id=6866999

80. http://www.nytimes.com/2009/08/21/business/21clunkers.html?_r=1

81. http://www.cato-at-liberty.org/cash-4-clunkers-fails-again/

82. http://www.npr.org/blogs/money/2010/09/02/129608251/cash-for-clunkers

83. http://www.nber.org/papers/w16351

84. [1]http://www.boston.com/bostonglobe/editorial_opinion/oped/articles/2010/09/01/clunkers_a_classic_government_folly/

85. http://www.toledofreepress.com/2011/06/03/presi-

dent-obama-addresses-toledo-chrysler-plant/

86. http://www.usatoday.com/money/autos/2011-06-03-chrysler-bailout-government_n.htm

87. http://www.factcheck.org/2011/06/chrysler-paid-in-full/

88. http://www.gao.gov/htext/d11471.html

89. http://www.whitehouse.gov/the_press_office/Remarks-by-the-President-and-Vice-President-at-Signing-of-the-American-Recovery-an

90. http://www.huffingtonpost.com/2012/01/03/child-poverty-20-percent_n_1181548.html?ref=business

91. http://www.reuters.com/article/2012/01/11/us-poverty-study-idUSTRE80A20H20120111

92. http://www.whitehouse.gov/the-press-office/2011/09/19/remarks-president-economic-growth-and-deficit-reduction

93. http://www.usatoday.com/money/perfi/taxes/story/2011-09-20/buffett-tax-millionaires/50480226/1

94. http://www.weeklystandard.com/blogs/top-01-per-cent-pays-more-income-tax-bottom-80-per-cent_594000.html

95. http://www.politifact.com/truth-o-meter/promises/obameter/promise/515/no-family-making-less-250000-will-see-any-form-tax/

96. http://republicans.waysandmeans.house.gov/UploadedFiles/DemTaxIncreases1.pdf

97. http://www.usnews.com/opinion/blogs/peter-roff/2009/04/02/obamas-cigarette-tax-puts-the-lie-to-his-no-new-taxes-pledge

98. Joint Committee on Taxation, "Estimated Revenue Effects of the Amendment in the Nature of a Substitute to H.R. 4872, the 'Reconciliation Act of 2010,' as Amended, in Combination with the Revenue Effects of H.R. 3590, the 'Patient Protection and Affordable Care Act ("PPACA"),' as Passed by the Senate, and Scheduled for Consideration by the House Committee on Rules on March 20, 2010," March 20, 2010, at http://www.jct.gov/publications.html?func=start-down&id=3672

99. http://www.dispatch.com/content/downloads/2011/03/16/Heritage-Foundation-on-health-care.pdf

100. http://www.presidency.ucsb.edu/ws/index.php?pid=85788&st=million&st1=homeowners#axzz1pOXoWq7p

101. http://online.wsj.com/article/SB1236176236021

29441.html

102. http://www.washingtonpost.com/business/econo-my/obamas-efforts-to-aid-homeowners-boost-hous-ing-market-fall-far-short-of-goals/2011/09/22/gIQAoJdeAM_print.html

103. http://www.chron.com/business/press-releases/arti-cle/Loans-org-Details-HARP-2-Guidelines-as-the-New-3399376.php

104. http://nation.foxnews.com/border-fence/2011/05/10/obama-claims-border-fence-basi-cally-complete-its-only-5-finished

105. http://www.cbsnews.com/8301-503544_162-20003600-503544.html

106. http://www.us-english.org/view/479

107. http://www.whitehouse.gov/the_press_office/Remarks-by-the-President-to-a-Joint-Session-of-Congress-on-Health-Care

108. http://cnsnews.com/news/article/hhs-obamacare-funded-health-centers-migrants-wont-check-immi-gration-status

109. http://www.whitehouse.gov/the_press_office/Joint-Press-Conference-With-President-Barack-Obama-And-President-Felipe-Calderon-Of-Mexico-4/16/2009/

110. http://www.foxnews.com/politics/2009/04/02/myth-percent-small-fraction-guns-mexico-come/

111. http://www.cbsnews.com/8301-31727_162-57338546-10391695/documents-atf-used-fast-and-furious-to-make-the-case-for-gun-regulations/

112. http://latimesblogs.latimes.com/nationnow/2011/12/fast-and-furious-atf-agents-death.html

113 [1]http://townhall.com/tipsheet/katiepavlich/2011/09/20/attorney_general_in_mexico_200_mur ders_result_of_operation_fast_and_furious

114 [1]http://www.cnbc.com/id/25084346/CNBC_Exclusive_CNBC_s_Chief_Washington_Correspon dent_John_Harwood_Sits_Down_with_Presidential _Candidate_Senator_Barack_Obama_Transcript_In cluded

115. http://cnsnews.com/news/article/obama-2008-sup-ported-gradual-adjustment-gas-prices-2012-doesn-t-want-higher-prices

116 [1]http://www.cnbc.com/id/25084346/CNBC_Exclusive_CNBC_s_Chief_Washington_Correspon dent_John_Harwood_Sits_Down_with_Presidential _Candidate_Senator_Barack_Obama_Transcript_In cluded

117. http://online.wsj.com/article/SB122904040307

499791.html

118. http://www.humanevents.com/article.php?id=
50085

119. http://energytomorrow.org/blog/drilling-down-into-
the-oil-reserves-numbers/#/type/all

120. http://www.newsmax.com/Limbaugh/Obama-Lies-
Big-Oil/2012/03/09/id/432004

121. http://www.instituteforenergyresearch.org/2012/
02/29/get-real-obama-the-spr-is-trapped-off-our-
coasts/

122. http://www.nationalreview.com/corner/293008/
how-obama-choking-us-oil-production-mario-loyola

123. http://www.whitehouse.gov/the-press-
office/2012/03/15/remarks-president-energy

124. http://www.weeklystandard.com/blogs/gas-price-
perfidy_633143.html?nopager=1

125. http://energytomorrow.org/blog/politics-energy-
and-the-president/#/type/all

126. http://www.whitehouse.gov/blog/2012/01/10/
president-obama-visits-epa

127. http://www.pacificlegal.org/page.aspx?pid=1652

128. http://www.politifact.com/truth-o-meter/promises/
obameter/promise/439/create-5-million-green-jobs/

129. http://oversight.house.gov/images/stories/Reports/9-
22-2011_Staff_Report_Obamas_Green_Energy_
Agenda_Destroys_Jobs.pdf

130. http://online.wsj.com/article/SB1000142405
297020452460457661191286160766.html

131. http://www.nytimes.com/2011/08/19/us/19
bcgreen.html?_r=3

132. http://en.wikiquote.org/wiki/Barack_Obama

133. http://www.washingtonpost.com/blogs/fact-check-
er/post/obamas-8000-in-gas-savings-a-year—oops-
over-a-cars-life/2012/03/08/gIQAhHiwzR_
blog.html

134. http://www.thetruthaboutcars.com/2012/03/presi-
dent-obama-says-new-cafe-standards-will-save-aver-
age-driver-8000-a-year/

135. http://www.nationalreview.com/articles/294232/
obama-flunks-math-nash-keune

136. http://www.issues2000.org/Archive/2010_House
_GOP_Energy_+_Oil.htm

137. http://hotair.com/archives/2008/11/02/obama-well-
bankrupt-any-new-coal-plants/

138. http://www.nytimes.com/gwire/2010/02/04/04
greenwire-sen-rockefeller-criticizes-obama-over-coal-
poli-5739.html

139. http://www.clipsandcomment.com/2008/08/17/

full-transcript-saddleback-presidential-forum-sen-barack-obama-john-mccain-moderated-by-rick-warren/

140. http://en.wikisource.org/wiki/Letter_to_the_Alice_B._Toklas_LGBT_Democratic_Club
141. http://www.cbn.com/CBNnews/446184.aspx
142. http://www.nrlc.org/News_and_Views/Aug08/nv081808part3.html
143. http://www.whitehouse.gov/the_press_office/News-Conference-by-the-President-July-22-2009
144. Pipes, Sally C., The Truth About ObamaCare (Perseus Books Group. 2010), 50.
145. Ibid., 51.
146. http://www.huffingtonpost.com/2011/07/14/ann-dunham-book-health-insurance_n_898192.html
147. http://www.washingtonpost.com/blogs/fact-checker/post/the-road-weve-traveled-a-misleading-account-of-obamas-mother-and-her-insurance-dispute/2012/03/18/gIQAdDd4KS_blog.html
148. http://www.politifact.com/truth-o-meter/statements/2011/jul/21/barack-obama/obamas-mother-fought-disability-coverage-not-treat/
149. http://www.washingtonpost.com/blogs/fact-checker/post/the-road-weve-traveled-a-misleading-account-of-obamas-mother-and-her-insurance-dispute/2012/03/18/gIQAdDd4KS_blog.html
150. http://blogs.abcnews.com/george/2009/09/obama-mandate-is-not-a-tax.html
151. http://abcnews.go.com/blogs/politics/2009/09/obama-mandate-is-not-a-tax/
152. http://www.commentarymagazine.com/topic/congressional-budget-office/
153. http://www.nytimes.com/2010/07/18/health/policy/18health.html
154. http://www.newjerseynewsroom.com/healthquest/obama-continues-to-push-health-care-reform
155. http://www.slate.com/articles/news_and_politics/history_lesson/2007/10/whos_afraid_of_socialized_medicine.html
156. http://www.cato.org/pubs/bp/bp108.pdf
157. http://www.newjerseynewsroom.com/healthquest/obama-continues-to-push-health-care-reform
158. http://www.youtube.com/watch?v=15E7goj7Fmo
159. http://blog.nj.com/njv_guest_blog/2011/10/president_obamas_health_care_l.html
160. http://www.ocregister.com/articles/health-334031-law-costs.html
161. http://www.youtube.com/watch?v=7Sk9kxaoLXM

69 Obama Lies

162. http://www.youtube.com/watch?v=7Sk9kxaoLXM

163. http://online.wsj.com/article/SB124597492337 757443.html

164. http://www.foxnews.com/story/0,2933,392962, 00.html

165. http://www.usatoday.com/news/washington/2009-06-15-obama-speech-text_N.htm

166. http://blog.heritage.org/2009/08/03/still-not-convinced-the-public-option-is-a-trojan-horse-for-single-payer/

167. http://www.verumserum.com/?p=6413

168. http://startthinkingright.wordpress.com/2009/08/04/exposed-obamas-lie-that-democrats-dont-want-government-takeover-of-health-care/

169. http://blogs.wsj.com/washwire/2009/07/22/excerpts-of-obamas-remarks-prepared-for-news-conference/

170. http://www.washingtonpost.com/opinions/coming-soon-a-bigger-costlier-obamacare/2011/06/14/AG4eAqXH_story.html

171. http://www.nytimes.com/2009/08/12/us/politics/12obama.text.html?pagewanted=all

172. Ferrara, Peter (2010-10-01). The ObamaCare Disaster: An Appraisal of the Patient Protection and Affordable Care Act (p. 12). The Heartland Institute. Kindle Edition.

173. http://www.whitehouse.gov/realitycheck/3 (starting at 1:08)

174 [1]http://www.mckinseyquarterly.com/Health_Care/Strategy_Analysis/How_US_health_care_reform_will_affect_employee_benefits_2813

175. http://americanactionforum.org/files/LaborMkts HCRAAF5-27-10.pdf

176. http://www.nrlc.org/press_releases_new/Release 090909.html

177. http://www.nrlc.org/press_releases_new/Release 072910.html

178. http://www.lifenews.com/2012/03/15/obamas-new-plan-for-abortion-on-demand-at-your-expense/

179. http://projects.washingtonpost.com/obama-speeches/speech/928/

180. http://www.cdc.gov/nchs/data/series/sr_23/sr23_029.pdf

181. http://cnsnews.com/news/article/obama-refuted-cdc-report-not-true-99-women-have-used-contraceptives-139-have-never-had

182. http://www.lifenews.com/2011/10/12/obama-threatens-to-veto-bill-for-no-abortion-in-obamacare/

183. http://www.hhs.gov/news/press/2012pres/01/

20120120a.html

184. http://www.whitehouse.gov/the_press_office/
ClosureOfGuantanamoDetentionFacilities/

185. http://www.jpost.com/International/Article.
aspx?id=249771

186. http://www.csmonitor.com/USA/Foreign-
Policy/2012/0304/Obama-to-AIPAC-I-have-Israel-
s-back

187. http://cnsnews.com/news/article/i-have-israels-back-
obama-tells-jewish-lobby-no-options-table-iran

188. http://www.haaretz.com/news/abbas-slams-obama-
for-saying-jerusalem-to-stay-israel-s-undivided-capi-
tal-1.247201

189. http://cnsnews.com/news/article/obama-again-
chooses-friday-afternoon-renew-jerusalem-embassy-
waiver

190. http://www.nytimes.com/2008/06/07/us/politics/
07obama.html

191. http://www.jihadwatch.org/2009/06/fjordman-to-
president-obama-regarding-islam-and-science.html

192. http://abcnews.go.com/Politics/OTUS/president-
obama-koran-apology-afghans-calmed-
things/story?id=15819707#.T2bwQ4FyhnQ

193. http://www.foxnews.com/world/2012/03/03/offi-
cial-says-mistakes-led-to-afghan-koran-burnings-as-
5-us-troops-may-face/

194. http://www.whitehouse.gov/the_press_office/
Statement-of-President-Barack-Obama-on-Release-
of-OLC-Memos

195. http://www.politico.com/static/PPM124_
ciadirsltr.html

196. http://www.washingtonpost.com/opinions/the-cias-
exoneration-and-holders-
reckoning/2011/07/04/gHQASrfnxH_story.html

197. http://www.reuters.com/article/2009/06/29/us-hon-
duras-usa-sb-idUKTRE55S5J220090629

198. http://online.wsj.com/article/SB100014240529
7020473180457438287271178415 0.html

199. http://schock.house.gov/UploadedFiles/Schock_
CRS_Report_Honduras_FINAL.pdf

200. http://www.nytimes.com/2009/06/04/us/politics/
04obama.text.html?pagewanted=all

201. http://www.huffingtonpost.com/2011/10/02/
dick-liz-cheney-obama-awlaki-apology_n_99
1062.html

Index

69 Obama Lies

Notes

Notes

Notes

Notes

Notes

Special Free Offer!

=======================

Two Tea Party Key Tags When You Stand Against The Left's Attacks

Take a personal stand against the Left's attacks on the Tea Party and Grassfire Nation will send you two "Don't Tread On Me" key tags as our free gift—one to keep and one to share.

The front features the "Don't Tread On Me" flag which has become the symbol of our movement while the reverse boldly states, "I Am The Tea Party."

Limit one set per citizen. Offer good only to patriotic citizens who uphold the Tea Party values of Liberty and Limited Government — and while supplies last.

Visit Grassfire.com/freekeytag to request your gifts.

Spread The Word By Ordering
69 Obama Lies In Bulk!

__ $20 for 10 COPIES

__ $30 for 20 COPIES

__ $50 for 50 COPIES

__ $100 for 100 COPIES

_____

First Name   *Last Name*

_____

Street Address

_____

City   *State*   *Zip*

(Credit Card form on back)

Call 866-GRASSFIRE or visit
Grassfire.com/69LiesBulk to order, you may also mail
your check (payable to "Grassfire") to:
Grassfire Nation, PO Box 277, Maxwell, IA 50161

Mail your check payable to "Grassfire" to: Grassfire Nation, PO Box 277, Maxwell, IA 50161

Please charge my credit card:

☐ MasterCard   ☐ VISA   ☐ AMEX   ☐ Discover

Card #:_____

Expiration Date: ___/___ Amount: $_____

Print name (as it appears on card):

_____

Authorized Signature (REQUIRED):

_____

Today's Date: _____

Get The "Tea Party Survival Guide"!

To survive and overcome the Left's blistering Anti-Tea Party strategy, Grassfire Nation's researchers have assembled the 2012 Tea Party Survival Guide — a pocket-sized powerhouse containing more than 140 pages of critical information and insight on what to expect and how to respond in the critical months ahead.

We've also included the U.S. Constitution and Declaration of Independence — all of which will empower you during this vital election season. Complete the form below to order your Survival Guides or call 866-GRASSFIRE.

___$_____ (any amount) for 2 COPIES

___$25 for 10 COPIES

___$45 for 20 COPIES

___$95 for 50 COPIES

___$150 for 150 COPIES

(Credit Card form on back)

Call 866-GRASSFIRE or visit Grassfire.com/BulkSurvivalGuide to order, you may also mail your check (payable to "Grassfire") to:
Grassfire Nation, PO Box 277, Maxwell, IA 50161

Mail your check payable to "Grassfire" to: Grassfire
Nation, PO Box 277, Maxwell, IA 50161

Please charge my credit card:

☐ MasterCard   ☐ VISA   ☐ AMEX   ☐ Discover

Card #:_____

Expiration Date: ___/___ Amount: $_____

Print name (as it appears on card):

_____

Authorized Signature (REQUIRED):

_____

Today's Date: _____

Obama Exposed

21 Ways Barack Obama Is Radically Re-Shaping America In His Own Image

Grassfire Nation

SEE OBAMA STRIPPED BARE. (HIS AGENDA, THAT IS.)

Obama Exposed is the blockbuster resource that lays out the 21 ways that Barack Obama has radically re-shaped America into his own image. In 64 compelling pages, you'll see how the son of Kenyan Muslim and a liberal socialist is implementing the most leftist political agenda our nation has ever seen.

Obama Exposed outlines the 21 ways Obama's worldview and policies are impacting your life, your family and our nation. And it's the perfect companion to 69 Lies. Complete the form below or call 866-GRASSFIRE.

___$10 for TWO copies.

___$20 for TEN copies

___$50 for FIFTY copies

___$75 for ONE-HUNDRED copies

(Credit Card form on back)

Call 866-GRASSFIRE or visit Grassfire.com/ObamaExposedBulk to order, you may also mail your check (payable to "Grassfire") to:

Mail your check payable to "Grassfire" to: Grassfire Nation, PO Box 277, Maxwell, IA 50161

Please charge my credit card:

☐ MasterCard   ☐ VISA   ☐ AMEX   ☐ Discover

Card #:_____

Expiration Date: ___/___ Amount: $_____

Print name (as it appears on card):

_____

Authorized Signature (REQUIRED):

_____

Today's Date: _____

Where More Tea Party Citizens Gather Every Day...

Every day, tens of thousands of Tea Party citizens come together at PatriotActionNework.com to chat, share, discuss, organize and strategize. One of the nation's fastest growing conservative social action networks, "PAN" offers all the social networking tools you'll find on Facebook in a forum that's just for us.

Launch your own full-service blog. Manage your home page and profile. Join online chats with other conservatives. Post in any dozens of forums. Join your state group. And that's just for starters. With hundreds of thousands of visitors every month, PAN is quickly becoming the online hub for Tea Party conservatives.

Go to PatriotActionNetwork and open your account today!